UNASHAMED ARTISTS

A Celebratory Miscellany on Advertising Art

Ruth Artmonsky

Published by Artmonsky Arts
Flat 1, 27 Henrietta Street
London WC2E 8NA
Telephone: 020 7240 8774
Email: artmonskyruth@gmail.com

ISBN 978-0-9573875-2-2

The cover design for this book is respectfully adapted
from the cover illustration for *Making a Poster* by Austin
Cooper, 1938, the frontispiece is a detail from the
Bridlington LNER poster by Frank Newbould, and the
endpapers are from the Cockade Portfolio.

Designed by Webb & Webb Design Limited
Printed in England by Northend Creative Print Solutions

ACKNOWLEDGEMENTS

This book, unlike my previous ones, has largely
been compiled from my own library, rather than
depending on the generosity and interest of
archivists. Apart from my long-suffering daughters,
Stella and Becky, and grand-daughter, Sally, who
have had to cope with my all-absorbing enthusiasm
for 'unashamed-artists', I have to thank David
Gentleman for the time he gave discussing his
father's work and loaning images; Eve Watson,
Head of Archives at the RSA; Anna Renton at the
London Transport Museum; and of course my book
designers, Brian Webb and Dan Smith, for their,
as ever, interest in the content of the book, which
allowed them the freedom for a certain amount of
cheeky additions, as well as great book design.

CONTENTS

"Stop! Stop!! I forgot to put my ticket in your litterbox!!!"

INTRODUCTION

'Your modern merchant prince is no Medici: he pays you money to sell his beans; and if you take his money, you've got to sell them, though your sensitivity be torn to ribbons, and your corduroys spotted with tears of shame.'

FRED.HORN, ART DIRECTOR,
T. BOOTH WADDICOR & PARTNERS LTD.

his miscellany of pieces on commercial art has been put together because time is running out – now into my 80s, for me there is neither the time, nor for that matter the market, to give credit to the many 'unashamed' yet 'unremembered' advertising artists that deserve to be written about, some even warranting lengthy monographs, for the contribution they made to the inter-war British graphic design scene – ergo these short pieces will have to do for the moment.

The miscellany is also a personal indulgence in nostalgia, for I have lived in Covent Garden for many years, and, retreating from its tsunami of coffee shops, retail outlets and Boris's bicycle racks, I live in my mind, in my local commercial art world of the 1920s and 1930s – at one time or another, within five minutes from

Tom Purvis, *Game Shot*, poster for Austin Reed, c.1930

my loft, were The Studio Ltd. [publishers of *Commercial Art* and *Art & Industry*]; The London Press Exchange and its associated studio, Publicity Arts; John Waddington, printers; *The Advertising World*; The Association of British Advertising Agents; Odhams, the printers; Outdoor Publicity Ltd. [that did just that]; Paul Derrick and Greenley's advertising agencies; and the Carlton Studios. Two of the most important artists' agencies – R.P. Gossop and A.E. Johnson – were actually in my very street, at numbers two and three. The rough rectangle, bounded by Oxford Street to the north, Kingsway to the east, the Strand to the south, and Charing Cross Road to the west, was a beehive of agencies, studios and printers.

In these pieces I have tended to dwell on biographical aspects of advertising art as much as upon design – why the artists chose the career paths they did, how they went about promoting their wares, who their patrons were, what sort of people they were, and so on. Characters appear in more than one piece so that by the end the reader will have in their mind a kind of macramé of commercial art in London in the inter-war years, with the occasional looking back into the pre-WWI years, occasionally moving forward to the post-WWII period. It is left to younger, more energetic researchers to write more comprehensively about the satisfactions to be derived from creating to commission, and of the artists who chose to do so.

A SNAPSHOT OF COMMERCIAL ART IN THE MID-1920s

'In France, indeed throughout the Continent, the poster-artist is given a free hand. He makes his designs, and woe-betide anyone who interferes with its artistic harmony. In short, art is the first thing to be considered, advertisement the second. In England, it is the other way about. The advertiser has no hesitation in altering, or making you alter your work to meet his views. He has no compunction in spoiling the artistic effect of a poster by needless lettering. He nullifies the effect you have aimed at, and then wonders that your posters do not bring him great returns.'

JOHN HASSALL, PRINCIPAL, THE NEW ART SCHOOL
AND SCHOOL OF POSTER DESIGN, 1905

 hether or not most poster artists felt themselves to be intimidated by commissioning advertisers in the early 20th century, as Hassall suggests, by the 1920s commercial artists were beginning to have more clout in England, and commercial art was beginning to have status as a valid profession. The more adventurous concerns such as the railways, London Transport and Shell were

Fred Taylor, *The Heart of the Empire*, poster for London Transport, 1923

demonstrating the advantages of using 'art' in their advertising and publicity; and the more confident artists and their agents were making stylistic advances in moving from merely producing pictures to which copy was attached to having integrated design where image, typography and copy formed a purposeful gestalt.

A snapshot of commercial art in the 1920s shows its rapid advancement in status, through the media of exhibitions, related journals and books, to the point where printers and advertising agencies were setting up their own studios, and groups of artists themselves banding into studios. Commerce and government alike were coming to appreciate the advantages in involving artists in more effectively getting their messages across to the public.

EXHIBITIONS

The major exhibition in Britain, mounted in the mid-1920s, was the British Empire Exhibition, which spread itself over some two hundred and sixteen acres at Wembley in 1924 and 1925. Its aim was primarily to foster Imperial trade, as well as to demonstrate the diversity, yet unity, of the Empire. Knight and Sabey, in their book on the Exhibition, describe it as:

Harold Nelson, *British Empire Exhibition*, postage stamp, 1924

Frank Newbould, *Tour the Empire at Wembley*, poster for the British Empire Exhibition, 1924

'without parallel in the history of mankind … Wembley throbbed with variegated life, with a vivid unforgettable realization of the Empire…'

Although dozens of commercial artists were to contribute to the 'graphics' required by such a show, the Exhibition did not have the design impact and influence of the Festival of Britain some twenty-seven years later, although both were mounted in a spirit of post-war revival.

Perhaps the best-remembered image of the Exhibition was its emblem – the Lion. This had been designed by F.C. Herrick, the head of the design studio of the Baynard Press, the firm that was to carry out much of the Exhibition's printing. *Commercial Art* in 1924 described the popularity of the emblem [Abram Games's emblematic head was to have a similar effect for the Festival of Britain]:

> *'The Lion speaks for the whole of the Empire and the whole exhibition; he was on the buildings, the posters, the notepaper, firms showing at Wembley used the lion in their advertisements as a shorthand…'*

S. Kennedy North, *British Empire Exhibition*, poster, 1924

This last was made possible by blocks of the image being available to exhibitors. The Lion was adopted beyond the Exhibition site and was to be significant in philatelic history, becoming the central image on the first commemorative British postage stamp. Five artists, including Eric Gill and Noel Rooke, were invited to submit designs, along with Harold Nelson. Although the Committee chose Gill's, the King intervened and Harold Nelson's designs won the day. Stuart Rose, in his history of British stamps, placed the Exhibition stamps within what he considered was the 'visual boredom' of British stamp design in the first half of the twentieth century. Whatever Rose's opinion of its appearance on stamps, the Lion served its purpose well and *Commercial Art* declared:

> *'Ask twenty people "What does Wembley suggest to you?" and nineteen of them will say "The Lion".'*

The paper consumption of the Exhibition was enormous – millions of folders and poster stamps, hundreds of thousands of posters and leaflets, and so on; and a considerable number of commercial artists were in demand. The main poster for the Exhibition just featured Herrick's lion, outlined, but the transport companies had their own posters, such as the London Transport map by Edward Bawden and Thomas Derrick, and LNER's 'Come to Wembley and be Happy' poster designed by Shep. A series of posters specifically related to the aims of the Exhibition were Spencer Pryse's 'Scenes of Empire', with subjects similar to those to be put out by the Empire Marketing Board.

But posters were given special exposure at the Exhibition, with a mixed nation show in the Palace of Arts and a British one in what was termed 'Poster Street' – an alley lying between the Palace of Arts and the Palace of Industry, consisting of some 240 ft of hoardings on which were hung some eight hundred posters. These cannot be considered entirely representative of poster art at the time, for the hoardings were hired out to firms who would obviously want to flaunt their own. The poster artists displayed included Fred Taylor, Tom Purvis, Lilian Hocknell, Edmund J. Sullivan, McKnight Kauffer and Septimus Scott, this last having his posters shown by four different companies. *Commercial Art* was fairly scathing about the standard, describing the Street as ' a gallery of pretty pictures without ideas', but commending the quality of the printing.

Opposite page: F.C. Herrick, *The Lion Symbol*, for the British Empire Exhibition, 1923

Herrick's symbol, is seen here applied to a souvenir programme for the Football Association Cup Final and on one of a series of advertisements for the exhibition by E. McKnight Kauffer, 1923

Kauffer, who was well represented at Wembley with a series of posters publicising the various sections of the Exhibition, was to dominate the poster show at the British Advertising Convention at Harrogate in 1924; *Commercial Art* gloomily predicted –

> *'These [conventionalists] will say there is too much Kauffer and will lift their eyes in consternation at having to look so hard for a Fred Taylor.'*

There was, in fact, a fair spread of styles at Harrogate, for, in addition to McKnight Kauffer, there were such individualists as Horace Taylor, Macdonald Gill, Aldo Cosmati, Frank Newbould,

Lovat Fraser, Dora Batty and Gregory Brown [whose four 16-sheet posters dominated the staircase to the exhibition]. British advertising conventions were to feature poster exhibitions from then onwards. By 1927 these had expanded from showing posters in rooms to having special hoardings erected, which surrounded each convention venue; for 1927 over sixty companies had their posters selected.

THE PUBLICATIONS

Commercial Art, the main showcase for this subject, began publication in 1922, owned by 'Commercial Art Ltd.'. The Studio Publications, which had been in existence from the 1890s, acquired *Commercial Art* and were to publish it – changing its name to *Commercial Art & Industry* and then, in 1936, to *Art & Industry* – through to 1959. It was to become the main vehicle of news and comment about the applied arts, particularly, in its early years, about graphic design and advertising.

The earliest volumes featured a series of articles entitled 'Artists who helped the Advertiser', providing brief biographies of artists and the publication considered worthy, at the time, to be singled out for commendation. Much of the work illustrated in the series could be described as 'historic' or merely illustrative – pictures that could easily have advertised other products or services, if supported by relevant copy, as with Edmund Sullivan's images for Selfridges or Septimus Scott's work generally. But it was evident, even in the early 1920s, that changes in style were afoot,

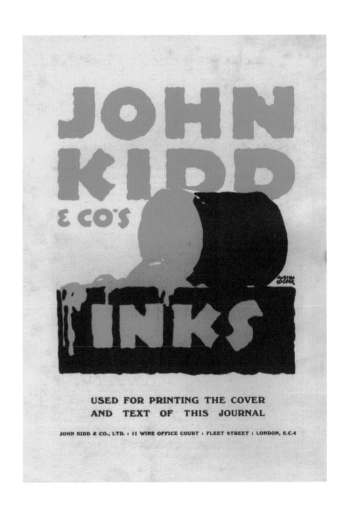

Austin Cooper, back cover advertisement, *Commercial Art*, 1924

14

Austin Cooper, cover illustration, *Commercial Art*, 1924

Tom Purvis, cover illustration, *Commercial Art*, 1924

F. Gregory Brown, cover illustration, *Commercial Art*, 1924

Frank Newbould, cover illustration, *Commercial Art*, 1925

with a Forster poster for 'White Horse Whisky' and, curiously, as much of the Zinkeisen sisters' work tended to be historical, Doris's striking poster for a theatrical production, and Anna's 'Rugby' poster for London Transport.

Further demonstrating that commercial art was establishing itself as a profession of proven validity, two books on art in advertising came out around 1924/5 – if not the first in Britain, then certainly the most comprehensive and influential. Walter Shaw Sparrow's *Advertising and British Art* was published by John Lane in 1924. Shaw Sparrow had studied at the Slade School of Fine Art in London and at the Académie Royale des Beaux-Arts in Brussels. He was to remain in Brussels some seven years trying to make his way as an artist and providing some articles for newspapers. In 1899 he became Assistant Art Editor for *The Studio*, and then went on to found his own publishing concern, for which he wrote books on art, architecture and interior design, but he is perhaps best known as a commentator on sporting artists.

Shaw Sparrow was a firm believer in the necessity to

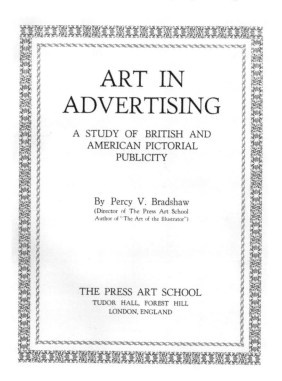

Title page, *Art in Advertising*, Percy Bradshaw, c.1925

improve advertising art, not, perhaps, viewing it so much from the perspective 'good art means good business' as in rather more crusading terms. Along Lethaby lines he saw art itself as a matter of 'good citizenship in honest workmanship'; and advertising itself, or rather 'good advertising', as 'lively and persuasive teaching by which knowledge is spread abroad quietly and amusingly'. He wrote in a totally eccentric, 'say it as it is' style, whether commending or criticising, which makes for refreshing reading amidst the generally platitudinous writings on advertising in the inter-war years.

Percy Bradshaw came from a rather different background. His book, *Art in Advertising* [undated], is generally considered to have been published around 1925. In his book Bradshaw gives an altogether more comprehensive and down-to-earth account of the scene at the time than Shaw Sparrow. It is perhaps relevant that he wrote not as someone with a fine art training, dabbling in the arts, but as someone who had been born in Hackney, left school at fourteen, worked in an advertising agency, and scraped together what training he could afford at evening classes. When Bradshaw came to decide to devote himself to art, it was not as a fine artist, but as a cartoonist for magazines and for postcards for Raphael Tuck. Bradshaw set up his Press Art School in 1905 and was to run it for some fifty years; and before summarising his experiences in, and opinions of, art in advertising, had published a series of monographs on illustrators, including H.M. Bateman, Heath Robinson, Spencer Pryse, Russell Flint and Edmund Sullivan. Bradshaw's large book, some five hundred pages, included not only accounts of notable advertising campaigns and the main commissioners of artists, but actually the brass tacks on how artists got their commissions – through artists' agents, advertising companies or artists' studios – and the printing aspects of advertising art. By its competence, balance, comprehensiveness and sheer readability, it should be a standard textbook for researchers in the history of British advertising art.

Other publications further signifying the growth of commercial art were the numerous booklets coming on to the market explaining 'how to do it', with titles such as 'Advertisement Design', 'Commercial Art Practice', and 'An Introduction to Advertising Illustration'.

THE PRINTERS

Commercial Art, in its role as commentator, was, from its start, critical of the output of the large, most reputable print houses handling advertising and publicity, complaining that even those 'with a fine modern plant with the latest devices' had not a man who was competent to lay out artistically.

Tom Purvis, addressing the Federation of Master Printers in 1931, and reflecting on his experiences in the 1920s, made a plea for them to employ artists, and generally gave a depressing picture of printers' 'artistic' efforts in the first quarter of the century:

> '…*poster designs were bought cheaply by the dozen…*
> *a poster design could be hawked around until it got*
> *dog-eared and sick and tired of itself, and finally some*
> *'mug' bought it – with great rejoicings on the part of the*
> *printer's salesmen. No name was put on the sketch…*
> *and generally the idea was just as bad for jam as it*
> *was for soap, and, if it sold for neither of these trades,*
> *it might go for shoes or tinned salmon or toothpaste.'*

If a client approached his printer, whose normal service was to produce his letter headings, invoice pads and the like, for an advertisement or poster, it would be standard practice for the printer to look through his stock of images to see whether there was anything at all appropriate, and, if not, to ring around artists he knew for them to send him in sketches. Speed was usually of the essence and producing something the slightest bit relevant to the brief within the time limit took precedence over quality or 'fitness for purpose'. A more positive example of this sort of touting by printers is given in a biography of John Hassall, sometimes described as the 'king of poster artists', who responded

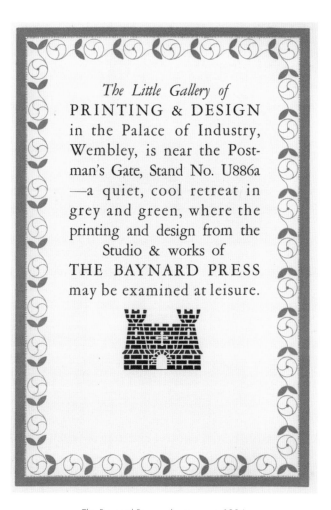

The Baynard Press, advertisement, 1924

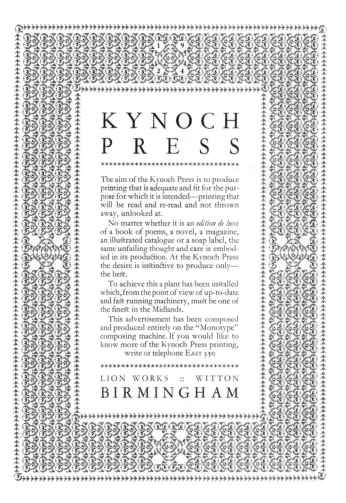

Kynoch Press, advertisement, 1924

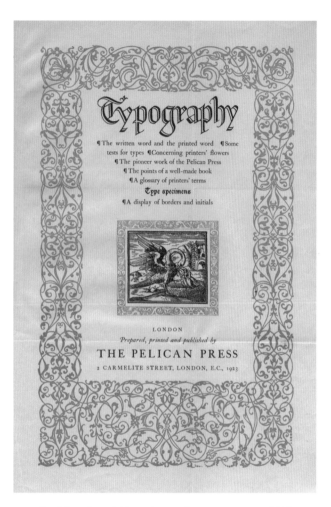

The Pelican Press, fold-out title page for type specimen, c.1925

to such a circular from Messrs. David Allen, a firm of colour printers, and, as a result, developed a business relationship with them which was to last some seven years, during which Hassall was to produce literally hundreds of posters for the printers.

Bradshaw wrote more optimistically than *Commercial Art* about the major printers of the time:

> *'[I] have long ceased to be surprised at finding*
> *that the heads of the principal presses are not only*
> *enthusiastic but men of fine artistic perception…'*

Of the ten examples he gives in his book, the majority were, in fact, being praised for their advertising typography – including H.W. Caslon Ltd., the Pelican Press and Francis Meynell at the Westminster Press. He only mentions two printers as having their own studios – the Curwen Press and Sanders, Phillips & Co, noting particularly the influence of the respective owners, Harold Curwen and Fred Phillips, both of whom served on several committees for poster exhibitions. The Curwen has already been extremely well documented. Alan Powers wrote of the Curwen, as it was in the mid-20s:

> *'The Curwen Press would sometimes deal with*
> *advertising agencies that were emerging…such as*
> *Crawfords or Stuarts, but it could also provide*
> *the same service directly for the client, bringing*
> *together copywriter and illustrator, and creating the*
> *physical artwork that combined text and image…'*

A key figure in the Curwen's use of artists was Joseph Thorp, who, at the time, used the Press at Plaistow for his own publications. It was Thorp who introduced the idea that Curwen should use artists, and, for a start, suggested Claud Lovat Fraser. Peyton Skipwith wrote of how Harold Curwen was so enamoured of Lovat Fraser's work that he bought one of his sketchbooks, with some two hundred designs, of which the Press was to make continuous use. But Harold Curwen and his Central London based colleague, Oliver Simon, went on to do most of the Press's searching for artists, and by 1925 Edward Bawden, a young graphic designer just out of the Royal College of Art, had become part of their stable.

Fred Phillips, of Sanders, Phillips & Co., sometimes known as the Baynard Press, was a printer with an aesthetic streak, particularly interested in 'fine press' books, of which he was a collector, having taken over the management of the family firm and set it on the path of fine printing. Joseph Thorp was again to play a part, introducing Fred Phillips to Fred Taylor, who, by 1925, was an established poster artist, and the two Freds became personal friends as well as working collaborators. Phillips appointed F.C. Herrick as head of the design studio he had set up. Herrick not only designed the 'Lion' emblem for the British Empire Exhibition but created the

Baynard Alphabet, which served as standard lettering throughout the Exhibition; and he was also to become a major poster artist for the period. By 1924 Phillips had also taken on 'Shep' [Charles Shepherd] who was to succeed Herrick as studio head.

ADVERTISING AGENCIES

Alfred Taylor, label for the Curwen Press

'The business man is not yet quite sure about the artist and the artist is not yet quite sure about the business man, though the conditions of the modern world demand that they cooperate. The artist thinks in terms of design and draughtsmanship, the business man in terms of sales and production. Without a guiding and organizing force the cross purposes might well become an insuperable obstacle. Here then lies the creative power of the agency.'

But then both artist and businessman were, additionally, suspicious of the agency, and rightly so, for in some cases they had started out as merely space sellers and had not been overly concerned about what filled the space. Even when agencies began to be aware of art as an asset to advertising, both art and copy were frequently misused. Buchanan-Taylor, J. Lyon's Advertising

ADVERTISING IS TO BUSINESS
WHAT WATER IS TO A PLANT
-NOT SO MUCH A TONIC AS
A NECESSITY

W.S. CRAWFORD LTD.
ADVERTISING
LONDON

Horace Taylor, advertisement for W.S. Crawford Ltd.

Manager, pointed out, in 1924, that the decision to adopt a national advertising slogan 'Truth in Advertising' suggested that advertising and its agents were in some way suspect.

Commercial Art, its focus on the artist and on the advertiser whose product or service was being advertised, had remarkably little to say about the intermediate role of the advertising agencies in its pages in the early 1920s. Its only pronouncement on the matter seems to have been in an issue in 1923 when it stated categorically:

> '*Every efficient advertising agency has its art director, whose functions are, roughly, to supervise the illustrating of every advertisement that goes out.*'

– but that rather begs the question of how many 'efficient' agencies there were at the time. Certainly there were a lot – the *Advertiser's Annual* of 1916 listed over two hundred in London alone – but few actually had their own studios. Bradshaw, ever optimistic and positive, wrote in confident tones that:

> '*The whole business of the advertising agent has grown more elaborate and ambitious, more responsible and reliable. The man with a glib tongue and facile pen, the aggressive "spell-binder" has been supplanted by the sincere, intelligent student of business and salesmanship.*'

And Bradshaw felt sufficiently confident that enough agencies were making good use of artists to include some twenty agencies in his book as worthy of note. He admitted that in the smaller agencies the owner would frequently do much of the work himself, but asserted that many of the larger ones were adding specialist art departments, not only employing their own staff artists but commissioning freelance ones.

Of the agencies he listed, Crawford's was perhaps the most progressive and influential. William Crawford himself was an enthusiast, with boundless energy for championing advertising, the employment of women in advertising, and the use of artists. In 1922 Crawford took into his office, as a trainee, the son of an acquaintance. So began the brilliant career, spent entirely at Crawford's, of Ashley Havinden [Ashley], one of the major graphic designers of the inter-war years. In his first year there the young Ashley accompanied Crawford on a visit to Germany and the resulting designs, especially those for Chrysler, were as challenging to the advertising industry as those of McKnight Kauffer. By 1929 Ashley had become Crawford's Art Director.

Among other notable examples of advertising agencies using artists in the early 1920s were Paul E. Derrick, who had been championing the use of artists since their foundation in 1894. Particularly remarked upon were their cheery advertisements for Johnnie Walker's whisky by Leo Cheney. The London Press Exchange produced a number of what were considered 'modernist' advertisements, an example being Gordon Nicholl's for Steinway pianos and Daimler Car Hire. Osborne-Peacock employed one of the most popular artists of the time, Septimus Scott, for their work for Horrock's Fabrics; and Stuart Menzies was in partnership with

Leo Cheney, *Johnnie Walker*, illustration for Paul E. Derrick

HISTORY IN A TEA CUP

A couple of hundred years or so ago we sold tea to the Nobility at £1 a pound.

The Smart Set in Queen Anne's reign creating a scandal by drinking tea for breakfast instead of ale.

Now, as then, we incur every danger to obtain the most perfect teas the world produces.

W.H. Hendy, commentary for Fortnum and Mason, c.1920s

W.H. Hendy for the Stuart Advertising Agency's iconic humorous publicity for Fortnum and Mason.

By 1928, the Advertising Association had affiliated to it such organisations as the British Poster Advertising Association, mounted annual poster exhibitions with its conventions, held poster competitions, and was supported in its activities by the likes of Leo Amery, Secretary for the Dominions, himself to be one of the major patrons of art in advertising with the striking posters and other publicity for the Empire Marketing Board.

ARTISTS' STUDIOS

By 1927 *Commercial Art* was describing what was becoming a common enterprise – the artists' studio:

> *'It has become quite usual for a small band of young artists to band themselves together, share expenses of rent, lighting etc., employ one of their number as chief salesman and get on with their job.'*

Typical of this description was the Bassett Gray Studio. Founded in 1923 by Charles Bassett and Milner Gray, gathering around them a number of young would-be artists and writers, many friends and ex-students from Goldsmith's College, the studio would eventually morph into the Industrial Design Partnership and finally into the Design Research Unit, one of the most dominant studios in post-WWII Britain. Shaw Sparrow was fairly scathing of artists' studios:

'Since the beginning of this century a good many semi-commercial studios have supplied advertisers with designs while passing young artists through the mill of daily experience. Their activity has proved that they have not been superfluous, but the ordinary standard of present-day work on our secret hoardings is a proof that they have not been very useful, except as a preliminary discipline for the young.'

However, the optimistic and pragmatic Bradshaw included a number of artists' studios in his book, considering the leading ones to be the Carlton Studios, the Norfolk Studios, and Publicity Arts. Carlton Studios was founded by two young Canadian artists – Archie Martin and W.T. Wallace – who, having already teamed up in Toronto, decided to set up a studio in London. They had complementary skills, Martin being an illustrator and Wallace a cartoonist, both with experience in press advertising and therefore considering they could offer a fairly broad range of service. They were said to have arrived in London with 'enough money to last six months and enough energy to last sixty years'. Touting their wares around, the pair soon accumulated enough commissions to take on assistants and to advertise what, at the time, must have been considerable rates – a catalogue illustration for a guinea or a really important illustration for from ten to thirty guineas.

AN EXAMPLE
Of THE WORK OF
THE BASSETT =
GRAY STUDIO WILL
OCCUPY THIS SPACE
MONTH BY MONTH

BASSETT · GRAY
IMPERIAL BUILDINGS
LUDGATE CIRCUS. E.C

TELEPHONE : CITY · NINE · FIVE · FIVE · NINE

Advertisement for Bassett-Gray Studios, 1924

Artists in Carlton Studios and examples of Carlton 'characters', c.1925

Their studio, with the rather grandiose name Carlton House, was divided into small partitions, so that each artist could have their own patch. In addition they provided, for everyone's use, models and costumes for figure work, a photographic studio, furnishings and fittings for sets, and a reference library. Carlton Studios eventually spawned their own trade magazine publishing company – The National Trade Press – and their own advertising agency – Carlton Publicity Ltd.

The Norfolk Studios were established in Fleet Street, but later on moved to Shoe Lane, in the City. They had been founded by Marcus Heber Smith as early as 1905, publicising themselves as 'The Home of Ideas for Advertisers' – not just artists prepared to execute the ideas of others but creative teams. Consequently, from the start, the studios had an Ideas and Service Department, along with their Art Department. The latter seems to have functioned with a degree of specialisation – 'figure men', letterers, and mechanical draughtsmen. They also seem to have had a pecking order for their artists, much as stylists in a hairdressers – with different rates accordingly. Bradshaw wrote of the studios' pricing policy:

'If the advertiser can pay a big price, he can secure a brilliant picture by a leading artist, but if the sketch he requires is not an elaborate one, or if the purpose for which it is to be used does not justify a large expenditure, he can still place the order through the same channel, and thus avoid delays and the trouble of hunting up different artists for different classes of work.'

By the mid-1920s the Norfolk Studios occupied three buildings with over one hundred artists and support staff.

Publicity Arts Ltd. was established just prior to WWI by H.E. Collett, an ex-Slade student, but one with his feet very much on the ground. Like other studios Publicity Arts had its own 'internal' artists but also drew on 'outside' freelance ones when necessary. Its business basis was rather different from that of other studios, for it found itself overwhelmed by commissions from two major advertising agencies – Paul E. Derrick and the London Press Exchange – and came to devote its services to the two, moving its studio near to the London Press Exchange offices in St Martin's Lane. In addition to providing artwork for the agencies, Publicity Arts undertook their printing as well. The studio had its own version of specialisation, not only typographers and artists, but, amongst the artists, 'colour' and 'black-and-white'.

The Crichton Studios, unmentioned by Bradshaw, nevertheless seems to have been a considerable player at the time. A leaflet which the studio included in *Advertising Display* in 1926 suggests a sophisticated understanding as to potential source of income:

'Believe me I'm a good advertising man. I'm au fait with the difficult art of idea-getting…I can so originate a folder that it will appeal to Sir Charles Higham, Mr.Hobson and the archaic Proprietor of Hannibal's Pills for Healthy People Or Mr.Taylor's Eno's…I am a member of Crichton Studios…'

Advertisement for Norfolk Studio Ltd. c.1920s

A Studio Advertisement without Illustration !

When you want art work done you have always got some pre-conceived idea in mind that you need illustrating, because an illustration of an idea, in the form of a picture, conveys that idea more instantaneously (if the picture is an illustration) than words can convey it.

Hence you want to give your instructions to someone with an intelligent conception of advertising and to someone who understands where art stands in its relationship to advertising. The more intelligent the grasp of the situation the more likely you are to get your idea intelligently illustrated in a clear, telling way ; the kind of illustration that conveys the idea behind the copy *in a flash*, with economy of line and effort, with pungency.

This is the kind of illustrative work we do for advertising. The grasp of your idea is there, and it is carried out with those little tricks of lay-out and technique which make the difference between getting this kind of thing *right* and just failing to get it right except at the third or fourth try. It gladdens the heart to work with a Studio which does work efficiently without the need to be constantly shown how this little device and that little trick of lay-out would make all the difference.

PUBLICITY ARTS LTD

Commercial Art

Sketches, designs and ideas for press, poster and window display advertising. Booklets, circulars and posters designed and printed. Commercial artists and our delegate friends from overseas interested in the Art side of Advertising will be heartily welcomed at the address below, by Mr. R. A. UPTON.

110 St. Martin's Lane, London, W.C.2

Advertisement for Publicity Arts Ltd., 1924

Illustrations by W. Smithson Broadhead for the London Press Exchange used in advertisements for Daimler Hire Services.

A problem facing researchers of how these early studios actually functioned was that the work invariably went out just under the studio name rather than that of the artist[s] involved, who were rarely acknowledged. Some odd occasional exceptions were Katherine Burrell in association with the Clement Dane Studio, Aubrey Jones with the Raleigh Studios and Garth Jones with the Norfolk Studios, but whether these actually worked within those studios or what the actual contractual arrangements were, is not at all clear.

In spite of the evident flourishing of artists' studios in the post-WWI years, *Commercial Art*, ever critical, was still suggesting in 1931 that businessmen were suspicious of groups of 'bohemian' artists selling their wares:

> *'The advertiser is too often mistrustful of the commercial studio. He feels that experimental ideas found amusing by a coterie of artists are demonstrably lacking in any serious sales dynamic. Sometimes, of course, he is merely short-sighted in this. Sometimes not.'*

To the commercial art historian, surveying the output of these studios in the 1920s, it might appear that there was, in fact, not enough experimental work, but that many of them were clinging cosily to Edwardian images in the face of the cold wind blowing in from the Continent.

ARTISTS' AGENTS

Percy Bradshaw described a competent artists' agent as something of a polymath:

> *'a completely equipped agent needs to be a lawyer, a merchant, an advertising agent, an income-tax expert and something of a diplomat as well as a salesman.'*

Artists' agents came on the scene at much the same time as art began to be appreciated as a possible asset to advertising. Four of the most important early agents operating in the 1920s were Francis & Mills, A.E. Johnson, Rogers & Co., and R.P. Gossop.

Although both advertiser and artist came to appreciate that a middleman was useful, if not essential, to their aims, this did not prevent both from begrudging the necessity of working through a go-between. Buyers of art for advertising – the advertisers – would frequently have preferred direct contact with their artists, not only because it would have saved them agency fees, but for the general ease of communication without having a gate-keeper translating their needs; and artists, in their turn, viewed agents with suspicion, particularly in relation to the amount they were obliged to pay for commissions.

Yet agents, and their apologists, could reasonably argue that many artists had neither the knowledge nor the temperament to work out beneficial contracts and, in any case, would prefer to spend their time creating rather than negotiating and dealing with paperwork. And when it came to art buyers, the agent could argue that often they had no clear idea of what was needed, little aesthetic appreciation, and thus were incapable of providing the artist with a clear brief, with consequent misunderstandings and delays. Further, the agent could claim a thorough knowledge of what was going on in art schools and in the art market and would be in a strong position to find the right person for any specific commission. And then there was the need to appreciate any artist's 'frailties' and 'sensitivities', referred to generally as 'the artistic temperament'. The agent could save the buyer the irritation and frustration that contact with such emotional beings might bring, the agent having the experience of knowing when to coax and woo and when to drive and threaten, and generally to act as project chaser and quality controller.

By the late 1920s there were over twenty artists' agents in London alone. A number of those who started up as agents came from an artistic background, for example Alan Francis of Francis & Mills, who had been a lithographic artist; others, such as A.E. Johnson, came from the media, in his case from Fleet Street. These early agents not only dealt with the works of their own artists but would buy in pictures that they would try to sell as they could – perhaps for illustrations or advertisements, perhaps for greetings cards. Rogers & Co. fanfared that they could supply anything from 'fine' art [a good deal of which was imported from Paris Salons] to what they termed 'graphic gymnastics', hinting that they were prepared to deal with works with 'a tinge of modernism'. Some artists' agents were prepared to extend their boundaries of operation to include display and exhibition commissions, and, later, to take on photographers.

Much of this gives a picture of agents as opportunistic and exploitive, out to get what they could from advertisers and artists alike. Yet there are many examples of close, fruitful and untroubled friendships between

Francis and Mills. Mabel Lucie Attwell, design for poster, c.1925

agents and their artists where both derived fair benefits. One such example was that of Mabel Lucie Attwell, who was noticed by the Francis & Mills agency soon after she had left St Martins School of Art and was trying to make her way selling the odd piece of art here and there. Francis & Mills took a gamble on her and provided her with a long and successful career.

When Alan Francis was joined by L.S. Mills in 1911, the pair undertook to keep their artists fully occupied, and later claimed to have originated the concept of a 'royalty' payments scheme for them. Besides Mabel Lucie Attwell, their best-known artist in the 1920s was Frank Newbould, the first President of the Poster Artists' Association and famed for his transport posters.

A.E. Johnson was particularly known for handling the work of 'humorous' artists, including H.M. Bateman and Heath Robinson; and the agency were also to carry sporting artists such as Lionel Edwards, and specialists in technical and shipping advertising such as Frank H. Mason. By the mid-1920s they had more than thirty artists on their books.

A.E. Johnson. H.M. Bateman, advertisement for Erasmic soap

Few of the artists registered with Rogers & Co. are remembered today, albeit the likes of Harold Foster and Smithson Broadhead were very well known at the time. In addition to British artists, Rogers & Co. also acted as agents for French artists through a relationship with French agencies. Percy Wall, Rogers & Co.'s Managing Director in the 1920s, had a special link to the Paris Salons, and was given advance viewing of works to be shown in case any interested him.

Reginald Percy Gossop was one of the most important agents in the inter-war years, besides himself being an artist of some note. Alec Davies in his book on Eric Fraser, one of Gossop's artists, described Gossop as someone:

'...*whose influence on advertising art in Britain – at times exercised from a position in the limelight, but more often from behind the scene – was great and beneficial over a period of many years.*'

And *Commercial Art*, in a 1927 review of one of Gossop's books, *Advertising Design*, wrote of him:

BETTER ART SERVICE

IF you feel the drawings you are using in your advertising are not giving all the value possible, give us an opportunity of helping you

❦ We have the services of many artists at our disposal, among others being :

Mr. W. Smithson Broadhead
Mr. S. Briault
Mr. John Campbell
Mr. H. Coller
Mr. C. P. Helck
Mr. H. Forster

Mr. F. Matania, R.I.
Mr. Gordon Nicoll
Mr. Tom Purvis
Mr. Balliol Salmon
Mr. Graham Simmons
Mr. Comerford Watson

We are sole agents for Nicoll Processes, Ltd., and can supply photographs, on paper, in full colour for commercial purposes

ROGERS & CO., ARTISTS' AGENTS LTD

ESTABLISHED 1906
INCORPORATED 1921

PERCY W. WALL
Managing Director

22 CHANCERY LANE · LONDON · W.C.2

Telephone - Holborn 558

Advertisement for Rogers & Co. Artists' Agents Ltd., 1923

'He was in the business of making fine advertisements when the idea was new to England and was personally responsible for much of the then pioneering work.'

Gossop's strength in offering to act as an agent for other artists was that he had experienced commercial art from a number of different angles – as an artist himself selling his wares, as a studio director selecting and managing artists in printing houses, and as an art editor. On leaving school in Grimsby he worked for a time as a general assistant to a designer, before trying his hand as a freelance artist. This was followed by a period at the printers Eyre & Spottiswoode, during which he took evening classes at various London art schools. By 1904 he had joined W.H. Smith and begun to build up its printing house studio. By taking on such artists as Fred Taylor and Septimus Scott, Smith's was to have what was described as 'the finest team of artists in the country'. Smith's in-house news-sheet applauded Gossop's energetic contribution:

'It would be difficult to attempt…to do justice to the influence of Mr. Gossop's work on the

Advertisement for R.P. Gossop, c.1930s

Firm's business…He says little, thinks a good deal, and does more…the best of good fellows.'

Gossop left Smith's to become the first Art Editor of *Vogue* in 1913, followed fairly swiftly by a further period in printing as Art Adviser to the Edinburgh printing house of Dobson Molle & Co. These rapid changes may well have been related to the onset of WWI, for by 1916 Gossop was involved in the distribution of printed propaganda for the government.

When the war ended Gossop started out in another direction becoming Joint Managing Director of the new Carlton Studios. However, this too did not last long as he soon left the studio on the grounds of ill health. It was not until his late forties that Gossop decided to set himself up as an artists' agent. He took rooms at 2 Henrietta Street in Covent Garden where, in 1923, he established R.P. Gossop Ltd. Over the years the office moved several times as the agency grew, finally settling in Great Russell Street where it remained until 1956. After Gossop's death in 1951, the agency was run by two women: his daughter, who had worked with the agency since 1925, and Kathleen Wilson, who became a director in 1948.

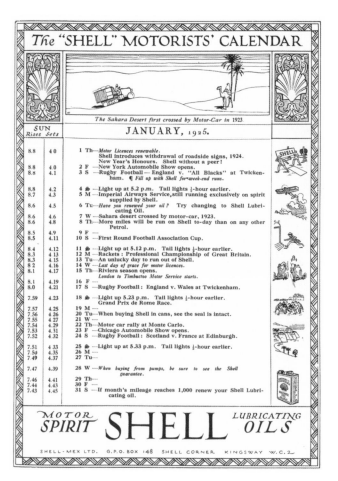

R.P.Gossop. Horace Taylor, press advertisement for Shell, 1925

Eric Ravilious, *Church under a Hill,* wood engraving, 1926

An early instance of Gossop as a 'fixer' was his organising, from 1926, exhibitions of woodcuts in the Basnett Gallery of the Bon Marché store in Liverpool, which included the works of the young Royal College of Art woodcutters, Douglas Percy Bliss, Eric Ravilious and Enid Marx. Gossop soon added to his original stable of Sullivan and Taylor a number of young talents who were, in time, to build up considerable reputations for themselves as commercial artists through Gossop's efforts on their behalf. By the early 1930s his 'list' included Dora Batty [one of the most prolific poster designers for London Transport]; Freda Beard and Irene Fawkes [both transport poster designers]; Nicolas Bentley [cartoonist, illustrator and author]; Austin Cooper [poster artist and Principal of the Reimann School in London]; Victor Reiganum [best-known for his book jackets and his work for *Radio Times*]; and Eric Fraser, probably the most famous, whose career Gossop handled throughout, both advertising commissions and illustrations for *Radio Times*. A Gossop advertisement for his services in 1927 also features the names Edward Bawden and Eric Ravilious, but these were probably included because of the Liverpool exhibitions. It is noteworthy that, of the thirty artists listed in this advertisement, about one third were women.

Gossop was an incorrigible writer of letters to the papers on all matters concerned with commercial art and design, causing a furor with one such which complained of the dreariness of British posters compared to the gaiety of the French ones. This led to a lengthy correspondence in which his main adversary was Tom Purvis, who wrote cuttingly:

'If an advertiser wants real spontaneity he can get it by going directly to the artist...thereby avoiding the possible mishandling by a possibly incompetent go-between.'

The best artists' agents of the inter-war years proved themselves to be anything but 'incompetent go-betweens', helping to build up the reputations of many of the major figures in commercial art, and, with many, forming long and fruitful friendships beyond any commercial contract.

An accurate if somewhat caricatured summary of the state of the commercial art scene in the 1920s appeared in the *Advertisers' Annual and Conventions Yearbook* of 1928:

'There is now a well-marked schism in the profession, which is divided into two opposing camps, the modernists and the naturalists. The modernists draw their inspiration from Continental schools, especially from the German. The Gebrauchsgrafik is their bible, Wilenski their chief prophet, and McKnight Kauffer their greatest exponent. On the other hand, the naturalists are still in the huge majority, Mr. Sep. E. Scott, Mr. Charles Harrison, Barribal, and a host of lesser lights are selling their pictures at high speed. It is probable that the naturalists are still the best sellers; they appeal both to the sentiment and humour, through either of which it is possible to touch the British pocket.'

FRED
TAYLOR

RELICS OF 20 CENTURIES
ENCIRCLED BY CITY WALLS

YORK

ILLUSTRATED GUIDE FREE
FROM TOWN CLERK, OR ANY L·N·E·R AGENCY

THE 'UNASHAMED ARTISTS'

FRED TAYLOR [1875–1963]

'Let us praise Fred Taylor for daring to be English and at the same time for doing something new and valuable.'

COMMERCIAL ART, 1928

Although Fred Taylor could in no way be rated the most progressive of 'unashamed' artists in the first half of the twentieth century, he was certainly one of the most prolific. He provided over seventy images for posters for London Transport alone, and his contribution to railway publicity has yet to be comprehensively counted, but certainly tops sixty.

Taylor was born in London. He showed early artistic ability at school, and on leaving at the age of sixteen he is reported to have joined a 'decorator'; exactly what the decorator did or what role Taylor played is not recorded, but it must have been useful to him, for it was some six or seven years later, at the age of twenty-three, in 1898, that he registered as an art student at

Goldsmith's College. He was to stay there for two years, gaining a travelling scholarship from the Painters' Company. This appears to have provided him with the means to travel in Italy for some three months, and there is also reference to his having spent some time at the Académie Julian in Paris.

After his travels Taylor worked for some time with Waring & Gillows Studio, under the supervision of Frank Murray, before branching out as a freelance artist. One of Taylor's earliest recorded posters was for the opening of Selfridges in 1909; and although he was to produce posters and other graphic work for a variety of companies, such as Armstrong-Siddeley, Thorneycroft's, Bechstein and Austin Reed, he can essentially be branded a 'transport' artist, designing not only for the railways and London Transport, his main clients, but for shipping: the Orient Line and the Royal Mail Steam Packet Company.

As with so many commercial artists in the 1910s and 1920s Taylor was fortunate enough to have two major patrons – Frank Pick at London Transport and William Teasdale at LNER. Taylor produced posters for London Transport throughout its various transmutations, from just prior to WWI, to just after the end of WWII – some forty years. Taylor venerated Pick, seeing him as virtually changing the poster world single-handed. One of

Fred Taylor, *York*, poster for LNER, 1924

Fred Taylor, drawing for Thornycroft publicity, 1923

Taylor's first posters for Pick, dated 1912 and advertising Sunday Concerts, portrayed both performers and audience, albeit he was to achieve fame for his fine draughtsmanship of buildings. Curiously enough, one of his last series of posters for London Transport, from 1942 onwards, again had non-architectural subject matter. 'Back Room Boys – They Also Serve' showed women tackling what had traditionally been men's work, wiring.

Taylor produced some exceptional work for London Transport for the British Empire Exhibition of 1924. His poster dated 1923, 'The Heart of the Empire', showed a view from Whitehall down to the Houses of Parliament and across the Thames to County Hall. He portrayed the scene as an aerial view, a technique he was to continue to use from time to time. The detail on this poster is remarkable and led *Commercial Art* to draw attention to:

'...his great gift for making elaborate and detailed compositions which are full of particular interest yet express a central idea.'

Taylor not only produced posters for the Exhibition but gave a week of his otherwise creative time to hanging examples of 'Art in Advertising' in its Palace of Arts; and some of his artwork was produced as tourist postcards for the Exhibition. Taylor had already tackled an Empire theme in his poster for the opening of Selfridges entitled 'Markets of the World', and into the 1920s he did a number of posters for the Empire Marketing Board, these showing the loading and unloading of cargoes, and suchlike. And Taylor continued with portraying 'Empire' in his mural for the Red Lacquer Room in the newly

Fred Taylor, *The Empire Shop*, Empire Marketing Board, 1923

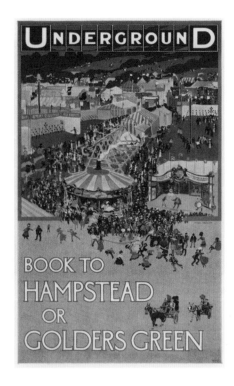

Fred Taylor, poster for London Transport, 1908

Fred Taylor, poster for London Transport, 1914

Fred Taylor, poster for LNER, 1924

built Austin Reed shop in Regent Street, which featured a state procession in India and a royal reception in East Africa. By the time Taylor was, at a much later date, yet again returning to the Empire, in a poster for the 1938 Empire Exhibition in Glasgow, 'modernism' had even begun to permeate his work, with his striking portrayal of the Exhibition Buildings.

William Teasdale, of LNER, was absolutely key to Taylor's prolific work for the railways, and the admiration was mutual between the two. When Teasdale selected his elite group of artists for LNER posters Taylor was preferred above the others, and consequently best paid. His most iconic poster for the company was of York Minster, of which *Commercial Art* in 1924 commented that 'it was probably the finest work of art ever stuck upon a hoarding'. The Lord Mayor of York said of Taylor's various York posters, that 'they will be preserved for generations'.

In 1929 Teasdale showed his appreciation of Taylor's work by choosing him as the first of the railway's artists to be given a solo exhibition. Herbert Morgan, a one-time President of the Society of Industrial Artists, who seems to have been blind to the romance of the railways, nevertheless appreciated Taylor's work:

> *'Apart from the architectural distinction of his work,*
> *his capacity to give colour and atmosphere to even a*
> *highly technical and detailed subject is remarkable.*
> *His massing of crowds and movement with such a*
> *dreary subject as a railway station is wonderful.'*

Taylor seems to have been able to build a close and trusting relationship with all his printers. He was to have his posters printed by dozens of different companies over the years, and relied heavily on their lithographic artisans, albeit he occasionally provided the lithography himself. He was perhaps closest to Thomas Griffits at Vincent Brooks, Day & Sons, and Fred Phillips of the Baynard Press. His trust of Griffits was such that one anecdote has him rushing away for a holiday in Italy and saying to Pick – 'Tommy Griffits can put all my errors or botches right. Why not leave him to do it?' Taylor had a lasting friendship with Phillips, and it is said that it was he who introduced Phillips to Pick, resulting in the Baynard Press providing print services for London Transport for some fifty years.

Much of Taylor's work was ephemeral, but his mural for Austin Reed and another for the Underwriting Room at Lloyds were to be seen for a number of years. The British Council holds some fourteen of his works and others are held in the V&A Museum. He is one of the relatively few 'unashamed' artists who has a photograph of himself [by Howard Coster] held in the National Portrait Gallery Archives.

Commercial Art summed up Taylor's attitude to his chosen career:

> *'Mr. Taylor is an enthusiast for his craft, which he*
> *has studied in all its phases. But not only does he*
> *know all about it, he also assumes that anybody*
> *who embraces his profession ought to devote all his*
> *energies to it in the same way as he himself has done.'*

Taylor was to remain 'enthusiastic' through to the 1940s when he was well into his sixties; an unashamed poster artist who, although early on somewhat overshadowed by the modernist artists McKnight Kauffer and Tom Purvis, and, towards the end of his productive life, by the next generation, Schleger and Games, nevertheless provided myriads of what were described as 'sure-footed, straightforward and robust images' that delighted the travelling public over the years.

Tom Gentleman, *Strange Church at Ayot St.Lawrence,* poster for Shell, 1937

TOM GENTLEMAN [1882–1966]

f Tom Gentleman's name crops up nowadays, he is usually remembered as David's father, and although, if he had lived long enough, he could well have been inordinately proud of his son's achievements, he himself was an artist of some note, with a career in which 'fine' and 'commercial' art ran on parallel paths. He can perhaps be described as only partially 'unashamed' in that, unlike some other artists, he doesn't seem to have been entirely comfortable with the compromises this necessitated.

Gentleman had none of the advantages that he was to provide for his son – a home in which both parents were artists and supportive of artistic ambitions. He was born in Coatbridge, an industrial town near Glasgow. His father, who ran a grocery shop, died when Tom was twelve, and the family assumed that he would not only continue to help around the shop but, on leaving school, take responsibility for it.

Tom had other plans. Soon after his father died he started attending the local art school on a part-time basis and, intent on becoming an artist, he not only got himself a place at the Glasgow School of Art but distinguished himself there, winning a travelling scholarship. His studies were interrupted by service in WWI, in which he was wounded fighting on the Western Front. At the end of the war he returned to his course and to take up his scholarship, travelling across Europe and into North Africa.

Gentleman had envisaged life as a painter, but although he was getting his work into exhibitions and solo shows, and

Tom Gentleman, poster for Shell, 1935

earning a little from cartooning for local newspapers, including the *Glasgow Evening Times*, he eventually decided that to get more remunerative commissions it would be necessary to relocate to London. He had the example of friends who had already gone there, including the Sangster sisters, who were working at Crawford's advertising agency.

Gentleman spent some time with several agencies – particularly Stuart's and Benson's – before himself joining Crawford's in the early 1930s. The commercial experience he gained enabled him then, through Stuart's, to join the Shell Design Studio as its manager, under the enthusiastic and inspirational leadership of Shell's Publicity Manager, Jack

Beddington. In this position Gentleman was expected to take on and develop artists, as well as working on assignments himself. He contributed to both strands of Shell publicity at the time – the nostalgic imagery of follies and landmarks [one Gentleman offering is of a subtly coloured 'Strange Church at Ayot St.Lawrence'] and the more edgy Kaufferesque modernist style, in which the typography was integral to the image [a Gentleman example being a poster of land speed competitions]. Gentleman had known Kauffer when both worked for Crawford's, and had been much taken with his work, as well as with that of the maestros, Cassandre and Carlu. As manager, Gentleman's work may not have been publicised as much as some of his more publicly known commissioned artists but his contribution to the Shell-Mex & BP Ltd exhibition of 'Pictures in Advertising' in 1938 showed that, in addition to his posters, he also worked on the company's written publicity. The two examples included in the exhibition, designed and illustrated by him, were 'As One Salesman to Another' and 'A Tale of Two Travellers'.

Of the artists Gentleman was to work with at Shell he particularly enjoyed both the cocky extroverted Barnett Freedman and the complex George Chapman; the latter was to leave Shell to become a full-time painter. It is possible that this could have influenced Gentleman to reduce his days in the studio to four, to allow himself time to pursue his own artistic interests.

With the onset of war, and petrol advertising put on hold, Gentleman was retained for a time by Shell, but then joined the likes of James Gardner, Pearl Falconer and Misha Black at the Ministry of Information. Gentleman's most striking works during the war were a set of remarkable 'safety' posters, warning of the potential dangers of moving around in the blackout. These were immediately eye-catching: blocks of intense blue and vivid pink, with figures made visible by carrying something white – clothing or a torch. At first the Ministry had over-generously opened its doors to all comers; but as it settled down to its purpose and worked out a realistic staffing policy, it began to make cutbacks. Gentleman was released in about 1943 and from then on, until his return to Shell in 1952, he worked in a freelance capacity.

Some of his freelance commissions came to him through the agents the Beaumont sisters, albeit he found this route had its frustrations as he would have much preferred to get both initial briefs and suggested amendments directly from the commissioning client. It is during this period that he again did work for Crawford's, for example advertisements for Maconchie Bros., pickle manufacturers, for the Electric Cable and Construction Co., and for Britannic Cables. He also found scope for returning to cartooning, with his covers for *World Review*; and provided murals for various clients, such as *Farmers' Weekly* [for the Bath & West Show] and Monsanto [for a British Industry Fair]. A major mural commission, obtained through Misha Black, was for the Kardomah Café in Rue de Rivoli in Paris. His brief was to produce a scene of a typical English garden at tea-time. Kardomah had previously given the brief to John Minton, but had found his draft too eccentric. Gentleman met the brief easily, and with delight, for it gave him the opportunity to draw freely, to include

Tom Gentleman, poster for Shell, 1936

Tom Gentleman, *Monsanto mural* for a British Industry Fair, 1930s

particularly easy, for although it gave him greater artistic freedom, the post-war years of austerity meant commissions were limited. He returned to the Shell Studio, but a good deal of the excitement and enthusiasm had gone with Beddington's departure to become a Director of Colman, Prentis & Varley. Gentleman retired in 1956, dying some ten years later. His career had been a fine balancing of home and work, of painting and commissioned work, of going along with the flow and striving for an individual voice. He was not to be as politically committed as his son, but nevertheless managed the odd bolshiness through his cartooning, and, in 1942, providing a poster for the Communist Party. The strength of his commercial work was recognised when he was made a Fellow of the Society of Industrial Artists; his paintings are held in public galleries, including the Hunterian Museum. On his retirement, the Shell Newsletter included an item that neatly sums up Gentleman's contribution to commercial art and his style of operating:

'Tom Gentleman's quiet but unhurried but firm insistence on good design and meticulous craftsmanship had a lasting influence on the Company's advertising. As a critic whose painstaking, and often witty judgement was respected, and whose frank kindliness was always the greatest encouragement to those who sought his advice, he will be missed by very many friends in the Company.'

figures in movement and rest for which he had a particular liking, and to covertly include those dear to him – his family, and even some horses, for which he had had a passion since childhood. He had just written and illustrated a book – *Brae Farm* – portraying an idyllic childhood on a farm in the Fair Isles; he had had an aunt and uncle with just such a farm, whom he had visited as a child. And again Gentleman was to return to sentiment in the lithograph he provided for Brenda Rawnsley's 'School Prints' series for schools in the late 1940s. In 'Grey Horses' he portrayed his hometown brewery horses with one of his small sons as onlooker.

Gentleman did not find this period of freelancing

FRANK NEWBOULD [1887–1951]

rank Newbould is best remembered as a poster artist for the travel industry – rail, shipping and underground. Born in Bradford, the son of a chemist, he trained at the Bradford College of Art, following this with a period at Camberwell School of Art. Little is recorded about his art school training or about what he intended to do on leaving. He does not seem to have committed himself to poster work immediately, but started out as a black-and-white illustrator, mainly for magazines. There is mention in *Commercial Art* in the early 1920s that he had worked for a printer, which experience it saw as consequently making him into a well-rounded artist, with a thorough knowledge of methods of reproduction and generally a businesslike, practical approach. Apparently he invested in an artists' studio in Fleet Street, albeit he himself seems to have worked in a separate studio in Kensington.

By the early 1920s Newbould was establishing himself as a formidable poster artist, providing posters for the British Empire Exhibition in 1924 and subsequently for the Empire Marketing Board. He had already been doing posters for London Transport from 1921, and for LNER from not long after the arrival of William Teasdale as their Advertising Officer in 1923. Whereas most of the artists providing posters for both London Transport and the railways tended to do their more progressive work for the former, Newbould appears to have bucked the trend. Even with his early work for LNER showing rural and coastal scenes he was using strong blocks

Frank Newbould, poster for Cunard, c.1924

Frank Newbould, poster for LNER, 1930

Frank Newbould, *Steel Manufacturing*, for the Empire Marketing Board, c.1927

Frank Newbould, *Jaffa*, for the Empire Marketing Board, c.1929

of colour with little detailing, yet by such simplicity he was able to evoke the sound of waves crashing on a beach, or threatening weather by a shadow on a hillside. Yet when he was commissioned to produce a poster announcing the installation of some technical advance, as with his 1932 poster of LNER electrical plant, he showed himself perfectly capable of providing sufficient detailing if it was required. In several of his offerings for LNER, particularly where the typography dominated the image, his work could be rated as 'modern' as that of McKnight Kauffer. His 'Harwich, a Gateway to the Continent' of 1937 might even be considered to be approaching the impact of a Cassandre. Newbould became one of Teasdale's 'elite five' – artists under contract to LNER.

Commissions he received from other transport organisations, such as Belgian Railways, the Royal Steam Packet Company and the Orient Line, show a similarly courageous attack. One Orient Line poster of a musician has only a long dash for his eyes and four dark lines for his finger separation on a stringed instrument, yet it immediately conjures up the exoticism of the Mediterranean for any would-be traveller.

In contrast, Newbould's work for London Transport was altogether more prosaic, more conventional and restrained, perhaps because of the smaller size of the posters, or, more probably, because of the subject matter he was assigned, along the themes of 'Blue Bell Time' and 'Harvest Time'. His destination

Frank Newbould, poster for LNER, c.1924

Frank Newbould, poster for London Transport, 1925

posters for London Transport, such as 'Waltham Cross' and 'Hadley Wood', tended more to his characteristic colour block style, but even these had a tinge of quaintness about them that does not inform his railway work.

Newbould did not produce any war-related posters during WWI, although he did do an RAF recruiting poster just after the war, in 1919; but in WWII he joined the War Office, about 1942, to work on propaganda posters. Although there is no account of his daily work round, there may well have been some awkwardness, for he, a poster artist of distinction, and of mature years, his mid-fifties, reported to a young upstart, one Abram Games, who was in his late twenties. In all, Newbould made some eleven posters for the War Office, four for the series 'Your Britain Fight for it Now'. In her biography of her father, Naomi Games, a shade unfairly, compares the clean modernity of her father's posters for the series with the rather old-worldliness of Newbould's. But this now seems an inevitability, for Games took to himself the designs that related to the future, with images of modernist architecture, whilst poor Newbould drew the short straw of having to illustrate a nostalgic rural Britain. The contrast between the two artists' images caused some stir in the Press along the lines of ' left-wing activism' versus ' conservatism'. Yet one has only to turn to the four posters Newbould did entitled 'Give us the tools…' to appreciate what he was still capable of achieving, even as one of the older generation. His image of black pliers crushing a swastika must be rated one of the most dramatic of WWII British propaganda posters.

Commenting on Newbould's career the Science & Picture Library has it that Newbould claimed to have started a new landscape school of posters. Certainly his LNER posters are striking for what the art historian Wilenski described as their 'gay colour' and 'forcible' design; whether they broke ground sufficiently to be described as 'a new school' is debatable, considering the remarkably progressive work of Tom Purvis, one of Newbould's contemporaries. Nevertheless, a number of his posters, for example the one for LNER showing the refuelling of the Flying Scotsman, and some of his War Office ones, remain clearly in the mind as coming from the hand of an individualist.

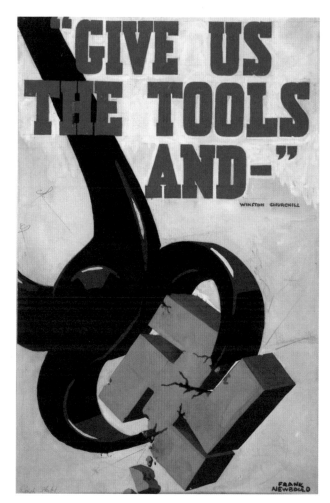

Frank Newbould, rough sketch for a poster for the War Office, 1940s

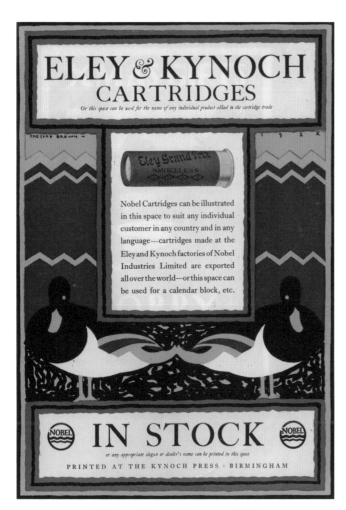

F. Gregory Brown, advertisement, 1923

F. GREGORY BROWN [1887–1941]

 Gregory Brown, [the F seems never to have been expanded except perhaps on official documents], was one of the most versatile of commercial artists, and certainly one of the most straight speaking, in the period prior to WWI through to WWII.

Gregory Brown was born in London, the son of an art teacher, albeit he always described himself as self-taught when it came to art. He certainly was painting from an early age, and by the time he was sixteen he had two paintings in an exhibition at the Whitechapel Art Gallery. Yet when he left school, rather than proceed to art college, he was apprenticed to an art metal worker, one Starkie Gardner. By the time he took up his apprenticeship Gardner was well-established, producing articles in a range of metals from iron to gold, including gates for the museum complex at South Kensington, and was a major consultant on art metal restoration as well as an historian on the subject. Such an apprenticeship would have provided Brown with considerably more than technical skills. Some critics have seen a link from the relatively simple forms and outlines of metal work to the style of Gregory Brown's art work. Such a link could well be argued as tenuous, but nevertheless his general approach to commissions was the practical one of an apprentice rather than that of an art student, for he was always concerned with such matters as how easily a design could be printed, and how economically, rather more than to what extent he was being given the freedom for artistic expression.

Eventually he began to find metal work rather restricting and altogether lacking in colour, and started to give more time to his painting, sending his works to many exhibitions. By the time he was in his mid-twenties he had been elected to the Royal Society of British Artists and had become a member of the Royal Institute of Oil Painters. Parallel to this he began to develop his career as a commercial artist. Shaw Sparrow, writing in 1924, described, in his quaint way of expressing himself, an aspect of this development:

'Some thirteen years ago he [Gregory Brown] was introduced by Brangwyn to the management of London Underground, and from that time he has confronted in many ways the problem of space-filling with rhythms of coloured pattern.'

F. Gregory Brown, advertisement for Cadbury's, 1921

Gregory Brown was to provide posters for London Transport, over seventy pieces in all, from about 1914 through to 1940. And certainly his style was a simplified one compared to many of the early transport posters. Not only did his countryside images lack detail but he began to dispense with outlines, even before this was done more strikingly by Tom Purvis. Shaw Sparrow went on to describe the style:

'Mr. Gregory Brown knows how to get surprisingly rich and varied effects with three or four printings. His flat tints form their pattern without the help of a connecting key of black outline, the effect being rather like that of stencil work.'

It is relevant that Shaw Sparrow used the term 'pattern', for Gregory Brown was experimenting, in these early years with textile design, winning a gold medal in the 1925 Paris Exhibition of Decorative Arts. But the textile phase does not seem to have lasted very long, albeit the 'rich and varied colours' and 'flat tints' were to become characteristic of his graphic work. *Commercial Art* was particularly impressed by the colour he used, writing in 1924:

'Using just a few colours in great purity and large masses, it has reached the highest peaks of daring in colour virtuosity.'

Along similar lines was an appreciation of a poster Gregory Brown did in 1927 for Southern Railway of Kent hop fields:

'The countryman who trails his heavy boots through the hopfields of Kent never saw a bark

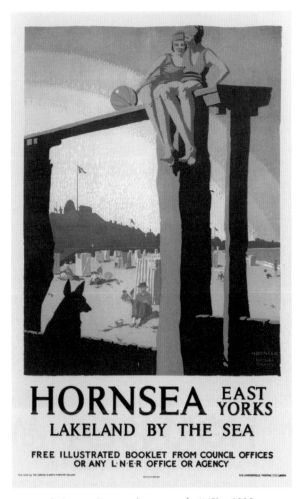

F. Gregory Brown, advertisement for LNER, c.1930

of an apple tree, the roof of an oast house, or the dust of the earth with such colours…'

Besides his preference for colour and simplicity, Gregory Brown saw himself essentially as a designer, and had a bee in his bonnet about the preference of early advertisers for using a piece of 'fine' art for their advertisements. His writing was full of homely axioms, and using one such he declared bluntly:

'A poster is a design, a picture is a thing to hang on the wall in a frame. There you have it.'

Not only did he see his commissions as designs but he was clearly aware of how type fitted in with image; this is particularly so in his work for MacFisheries, Nobel Industries, and Bobby & Co. although the type rarely overlaps – except when it came to his signature, which stood out boldly in all his work!

Gregory Brown can be seen to be an early 'modernist', not only in his work, for which he declared that 'subtleties were out of place', but in his life-style. His Hampstead home was described as a 'designer' house, with an up-to-date studio, which attracted another axiom – 'the way a man looks at life is revealed in his art'. He seems to have had considerable self-assurance about how he lived, how he created, and the value of his output. By the mid-1920s he had mounted at least two solo exhibitions of his posters – one at the Burlington Galleries and another at the Architectural Association. But Gregory Brown was energetic

F. Gregory Brown's 'up-to-date' studio in Hampstead, 1925

F. Gregory Brown, showcard design for Hope & Sons, 1923

on behalf of his colleagues' work as well as his own, defending 'commercial art' as a valid outlet for talent. He wrote frequently on the subject, along the lines:

> *'Is it less worthy to design a good carpet or a good cup or a good advertisement than to paint a picture?'*

and further:

> *'If art is to be a living force, it must break the bounds of the picture frame, it must reach the things of everyday life…Truly catholic art must apply itself towards the improving the lives of people and their surroundings.'*

In his crusade to democratise art Gregory Brown even took on the mighty Design & Industries Association [of which he is sometimes mistakenly described as a founder member]. An article he wrote in the *Quarterly Journal* in 1928 stimulated a good deal of correspondence, mainly hostile. He had started with stating his own ethical position when it came to taking a commission:

> *'I do not aid any industry run in opposition to the common good, nor do I encourage design as a means of extorting higher prices from a long-suffering public.'*

But went on, with some nerve and principle, if with a degree of foolhardiness, to target the DIA membership itself:

*'High priests of the DIA sell their everyday things at
prices at least twice as high as the article's value…and…
completely beyond the reach of the general public.'*

The cat was amongst the pigeons! Yet his argument had
some strength – good design is paramount but not if it is only
accessible to an elite – an argument that could be applied to William
Morris's products and those of the Bloomsbury set's Omega
workshop amongst a myriad of similar well-meaning middle-class
projects. The passion with which Gregory Brown wrote and spoke
about his mission was noted by *Commercial Art*:

*'To hear him wax eloquent on the need for bringing art
right into the heart of everyday life is to receive a new
and rare appreciation of the function of commercial art.'*

Gregory Brown's colourful images were to serve a vast range
of goods from blankets to carpet sweepers, from plays to textiles to
cartridges. His graphic work for MacFisheries was rated as not only
boosting the firm's balance sheet but raising the status of an entire
industry. Although only a shade less modernist than McKnight
Kauffer, by the 1930s Gregory Brown was almost entirely eclipsed
by him, and is nowadays barely remembered, even by those
interested in the history of advertising design. Yet his work is held in
a number of collections and photographs of him by Howard Coster
are in the National Portrait Gallery archives – a recognition held by
few of the country's 'unashamed' artists.

F. Gregory Brown, poster for *Ideal Home Magazine*, 1930s

HUMOUR IN ADVERTISING
FOUGASSE AND OTHERS

lthough 'art in advertising' is commonly traced back to 'Bubbles' for Pears Soap in 1886, the use of humour, and, in particular, the commissioning of cartoonists for advertising, lagged a good deal behind. There is the odd example of such use prior to WWI, but 'fun' was not used very much for advertising wares and services until the years following the war; it was not until the 1920s that humour can be said to have become a prevalent characteristic of British advertising.

There seems to have been a general wariness about whether making one's product a butt for jokes would not be shooting oneself in the foot; and there were additional murmurs about breaking the boundaries of 'good taste' – of the humour being used as possibly 'doubtful' if not actually 'offensive'. As late as 1927 *Commercial Art* was arguing that it was the social reticence of the British that made them hesitant:

> *'In dealing with comparative strangers most English people hesitate to venture beyond the ordinary amenities into positive mirth-provoking forms of speech or behaviour; and naturally this racial characteristic has had its effect on British advertising.'*

John Hassall is one of the earliest artists to have introduced humour into his work, just prior to WWI. Working for the agency David Allen & Sons, he produced one of the first humorous posters, 'Skegness is so Bracing', in 1908. By 1909 he was running his own school of poster design in Kensington, which was attended by some of the best names in humorous advertising of the next generation, including H.M. Bateman. By the early 1920s Hassall had been branded 'the king of humorous posters' and, at about the same time, a number of companies began to test the water by introducing fun into their press advertisements. Connolly Bros., although a relatively small firm, produced a series of publicity handbooks designed by such artists as Heath Robinson, Alfred Leete [of 'Your Country Needs You' fame], David Gilchik, Harry Rountree and Fougasse; whilst J.W.B. Cassels, the advertising manager of Moss Bros., was also making use of Heath Robinson and Bateman in his targeted advertising to the firm's clientele in the hunting and military fraternity, along the lines that they would look ridiculous in their respective fields unless dressed by Moss Bros.

But the major exponents of the ability of humour to sell, in the inter-war years, were Guinness, Shell and Fortnum & Mason, all of which have been extremely fully documented. Shell made rather more use of humour in their press advertisements than in their posters, although by the time the more earthy John Reynolds had replaced Rex Whistler [who was considered to lack a common touch], the theme 'That's Shell – That was' had crept into their lorry bills. Not only did Shell commission some of the artists Connolly had used but by the late 1920s they had even persuaded Anna Zinkeisen [perhaps not best remembered for her humorous pieces]

H.M. Bateman, advertisement for The Nickeloid Electrotype Co. Ltd., 1924

to join the merry throng. Charles Knight, taking a critical look at what was going on at Shell, commented:

> *'There is a lightness and liveliness about*
> *Shell advertising which is peculiarly*
> *appropriate to so versatile a product.'*

Yet Shell were always to hedge their bets, for at the same time as they were getting Bateman to pen his car drivers filling up their tanks, they were using the fairly conventional oils and lithographs of Fouqueray to picture Loch Lomond, Beachy Head and other splendid venues reachable by cars carrying Shell petrol; and, of course, this vein was further mined by Jack Beddington into the 1930s with his prolifically commissioned scenes of follies and ruins and the like, only leavened by Bawden and others with their puns on town names – 'Great Snoring' and other such whimsy.

It was Stuart Menzies who was to put Fortnum & Mason on the humorous track in the mid-1920s, although he claimed there was no way he would have dared without the 'boldness and breadth of vision' of Colonel C.E. Wyld, who was then fully in charge of the firm after his spell in the King's Royal Rifles in the war. Menzies suggested that, because of the 'exclusive' nature of F&M's clientele, it should use focused direct mailing rather than press advertising:

> *'I visualize little booklets, sent to a carefully*
> *chosen mailing list; booklets as readable as*
> *something bought at a bookstall or drawn from*

H.M Bateman, advertisement for Shell, 1923

60

a library. Every preconceived notion of a trade catalogue was to be violated. Space was to be sacrificed to pure fun in every direction.'

With this in mind, Menzies started on his 'Commentaries', the name he gave to his booklets, and space there was not – every inch of every page was filled with Menzies' copy accompanied by the illustrations of W.H. Hendy. Few edible products eluded the wit of the pair – from plum cake and stilton to oysters and asparagus. The Curwen Press was carrying out some of the printing for Menzies and, by the 1930s, Edward Bawden, who had done work for Curwen, was drawn into the fun through Menzies' Stuart Agency, and later through Colman, Prentis & Varley, who followed them as F&M agents. The rest, as they say, is history, a Bawden history, delightfully recorded by Peyton Skipwith in his *Entertaining à la Carte*. 'Commentaries' were replaced by catalogues to amuse the still select clientele, Bawden eventually working with Ruth Gill and her copywriters, as Hendy had done with Menzies.

Fougasse, who was used by both Connolly Bros. and Shell, started producing his cartoons for advertising at much the same time as Bateman. Largely remembered for his many years of association with *Punch* and for his wartime work with various government departments, particularly his 'Careless talk costs lives' series, Fougasse did a good deal of commercial work as well. Austin Reed of Regent Street once said that they were lucky to get Fougasse to work for them at all as 'few business men could persuade Bird [Fougasse's real name] to lend his skills to promoting their product'.

Bolshie Lobster attempting to Belt an Earl

Commentary on
D·A·I·N·T·I·E·S
to fit you for the
Stress of Autumn

WRITTEN AND PREPARED BY FORTNUM AND MASON

instructions for use of Commentary
Guaranteed free from colouring matter or exaggerations of any kind. Highly recommended to nursing mothers after being well shaken

182 Piccadilly W1   Phone Regent 0040

W.H. Hendy, commentary for Fortnum and Mason, c.1930

Fougasse, advertisement for Austin Reed, 1935

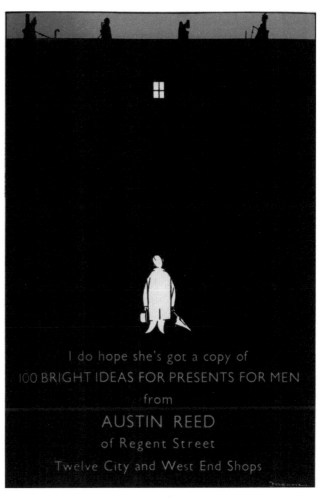

Fougasse, advertisement for Austin Reed, 1935

Fougasse, advertisement for Austin Reed, 1930s

James Taylor, who wrote a short biography of Fougasse, claimed that commercial commissions were not his preferred area of work, and allocated only a couple of pages and half a dozen illustrations to Fougasse's commercial output. Yet, on these same pages, on which he had been rather dismissive of such work, Taylor could write:

'He promoted a mind-boggling range of goods, products and services including bacon, cameras, cigarettes, chocolates, custard powder, electricity, fireworks, insurance, peas, petrol, air and rail travel, soup, tea, vacuum cleaners and whisky.'

It is probable that all Fougasse's commercial work put together cannot match his prolific work for *Punch*, but nevertheless it warrants more than a passing nod.

Cyril Kenneth Bird was an exceptional young man. Born in Paddington in 1887, he was not only gifted artistically but a good sportsman [a competitive boxer, and a rugger player to a professional level] and, in fact, an outstanding personality [Head

"I'm afraid you'll have to shout — I make so much noise I can't hear a thing."

CLATTER DOES MATTER

Fougasse, advertisement for the Ministry of Information, 1940s

Boy at Cheltenham College and President of the Union at King's College, London, where he read Civil Engineering]. He studied this subject somewhat reluctantly, to please his parents, as he would have preferred to be at art school, and, indeed, whilst he was working as a civil engineer, he attended various art evening classes at Regent Street Polytechnic and at the School of Photo-Engraving at Bolt Court. It was as if he was building up his courage to break free, but, fortunately or unfortunately, it was a disaster that pushed him to make the career change.

Fougasse joined the Royal Engineers as a sapper subaltern at the start of WWI and was sent to Gallipoli in 1915. There a shell shattered his back so that he had to spend some three years in hospital, and it was nearly fives years before he could walk again easily. It was perhaps curious that he chose the pseudonym 'Fougasse' [a French mine], but it was not so much for its wartime association as for its unreliability – there was no knowing when it would go off, and that's how he was reported feeling about his cartoons. It was whilst he was recuperating that his wife, herself an artist, encouraged him to draw, or rather to doodle. By 1916 he had his first cartoon accepted by *Punch*, a modest event in itself, but one which led to his becoming a steady contributor and, eventually, the magazine's art editor in 1937, and its editor in 1949.

Meanwhile Fougasse worked on dozens of advertising commissions, mainly obtained through his agent A.E. Johnson, who came to specialise in humorous artists, handling the entire work of Heath Robinson and Bateman as well. Perhaps with more than a degree of self-interest, Johnson wrote in 1921:

'It is less than four years since the first Fougasse drawings appeared, and seldom, if ever, has a humorous artist made good in so brief a space of time.'

In the 1920s Fougasse supplied work for, amongst others, Abdullah Cigarettes, Imperial Airways, Connolly Bros., Tootal Broadhurst, and London Transport. A rare early poster for LNER was not in the form of a cartoon and suggests the strength of conventional image he was capable of achieving had he not chosen cartooning as his métier.

Fougasse's perhaps best-remembered commercial work was for Austin Reed, the outfitters. Throughout the 1930s Fougasse's 'whispering men' were to be seen on much of the firm's publicity, along with targeted cartooning such as 'Start your Holiday at Austin Reed'. His drawings for their series 'Man about Regent Street' were so popular that they were later made into a book. In all, he is thought to have provided for the company over two hundred press advertisements and some ten posters; and eventually five books of compilations were published. By the mid-1930s plaudits were received from all directions. The *Print User's Year Book* was particularly enthusiastic:

'If brevity be the breath of wit, then Fougasse is the wittiest of them all. His work for Austin Reed's small spaces is as rich in humour as it is sparse in line. Here…we get a happy wedding of graphic and verbal art.'

THE MAN WHO LOST HIS CORKSCREW—!

H.M. Bateman, illustration for H.B. Fearon & Son wine merchants, 1924

W. Heath Robinson, *Heath Robinson's Idea of Comfort*, advertisement for Comfort Soap, 1924

And 'brevity' and 'sparseness' aptly describe Fougasse's images. Whatever it was that he took from his early influences – Phil May, the *Punch* artist Dumb Crambo, and the Frenchman, Caran d'Ache – he pared his own humour down to an absolute minimum, both in image and in word. And yet his simple outlines, with the occasional dot for a nose, a small dash for a mouth, a mere circle and dot for an eye, not only told the whole story, but became immediately recognisable as from Fougasse's hand, and no other.

The simplicity of his work at first suggests that he worked spontaneously, just dashing an idea down in a minute; yet descriptions of how he went about a commission show him to have been a careful, thoughtful worker, making numerous attempts to catch just the right look or emotion, and it was said that he never drew a final version straight off. When asked why his figures were so simple, he replied that the more realistic, the more true-to-life a drawing, the less was its versatility; whereas his 'formula' men and women could represent 'everyman' in any situation.

Fougasse not only deliberately refined his own 'handwriting' but made a positive decision when he chose cartooning for his messages. In a conversation with Percy Bradshaw, whose Press Art School correspondence course he had taken as a young civil engineer, Fougasse attempted to explain his seriousness in being funny:

> '...most of us do not readily recognize the difference between genuine humour and facetiousness. A jibe needs to keep its feet on the ground – its footprints ought to leave a definite impression. It must be related, however lightly, to reality; it mustn't just float away into the air the moment it is delivered.'

Fougasse did the bulk of his commercial work prior to WWII. During the war he occupied himself by supplying myriads of cartoons to aid the war effort – urging the populace to economise, to avoid waste, to save more, to conserve fuel, to avoid 'careless talk', and so on. His targeted wit was rewarded with an MBE in 1946. After the war he became preoccupied with *Punch*, and continued compiling his cartoons into books, some twenty or so in all; his commercial promotional work was behind him. He died in 1965.

Tom Purvis, poster for Shell, 1928

TOM PURVIS [1888–1959]

'Of Tom Purvis one can truly say that he knows his job from beginning to end, and that he observes all that is worth observing appertaining to his profession. Gifted with a fine visual memory, with imagination and with a great faculty of expression this versatile artist is undoubtedly one of the forces of the art world, and one that business men are well advised to take into full account…if there were a University of Advertising he should be its first Professor of Commercial Art.'

COMMERCIAL ART, OCTOBER 1924

 n an article in *The Times* in 1978, Bevis Hillier regretted that there was, at the time, no book on Tom Purvis, and that no one had mounted any kind of retrospective of his work. After a lapse of nearly twenty years, a small exhibition was in fact mounted in 1996 at the National Railway Museum in York; and in the same year John Hewitt wrote a comprehensively researched but only modestly produced booklet on Purvis, of some twenty-seven pages with only around twenty illustrations.

Such underwhelming exposure is curious, for not only was Purvis one of the most prolific of inter-war designers of posters and press advertisements, but one whose individualistic style was as immediately recognisable as that of McKnight Kauffer. Whether one has a picture of Purvis similar to that given by Ashley Havinden, 'a John Bull, sturdy, strong-legged, taciturn and essentially solid', or one more akin to Hillier's description of Purvis as a jovial clubman, a popular after-dinner speaker, a showy Lancia driver, and an occasional mouth organ player, it is clear that Purvis was no shy violet avoiding the limelight and consequently likely to fall below the radar of graphic design historians.

John Hewitt rated him as only a compromiser to clients' needs, but for that very reason a typical model of a commercial artist of the time, generally useful in illustrating how commercial art developed in the inter-war period. It is true that much of Purvis's early work was sentimentally realistic, in both subject matter and treatment, as was the custom of the time, but even with some of his early designs a tendency towards simplification is discernible, demonstrating not only the influence of the Beggarstaff Brothers, whom he greatly admired, but his own emerging attraction towards block colour and minimal detailing without outline, characteristics that were to be his trademark.

Purvis was born in Bristol but brought up in London. His father, an ex-mariner, had turned marine artist, and much of Purvis's youth was spent generally helping out in his father's studio:

> *'quite in the fashion of the ancients, cleaning brushes …priming canvases, mixing colours, learning strict economy in the use of materials, and, above all, learning the discipline and full use of a hard day's work.'*

In return for his 'hard work' and enthusiasm, his father offered him some financial support when Purvis decided on a career in art. This, along with some scholarship money and what he could earn from small commissions, saw him through three and a half years at Camberwell School of Art. Looking back, he was to be fairly scathing of art school training as a basis for earning one's living as a commercial artist, and was to become evangelical on the subject. However, he did not waste time, and, with a remarkable maturity, he set about getting the kind of training he felt was more relevant:

> *'For want of such help it cost me*
> *over six years to learn something*
> *of art in advertising from the*
> *inside of an agency…'*

The agency was Mather & Crowther, and it was there that Purvis produced his earliest known work, an advertisement for Dewar's whisky. His years with the agency can be considered his apprenticeship, and this he seems to have appreciated, for, when he considered he had come to a point at which he knew more than his boss, he decided to supplement his want of technical experience by a period with a firm of printers, the Avenue Press. There can be few art students at the time who went straight from college to an advertising agency and then

Tom Purvis, poster for the Avenue Press, 1924

on to train in lithography at a press. Some of Purvis's work came through advertising agencies, as when S.H. Benson commissioned the Avenue Press to both design and print advertising for their campaigns for Bovril. When, with hindsight, one considers Purvis's later preference for block colour design, it is tempting to relate this to his learning the process of colour lithography, where there would be a black outline template with a number of coloured overlays; in Purvis's case he would appear to have discarded the black outlines.

Purvis's career was interrupted by his service in the Artists' Rifles during WWI. Just as he had immersed himself in the most routine aspects of commercial art, he was to be the most diligent of servicemen, and was rewarded with a commission. He was not to return to designing until 1919, but by then he seems to have considered himself completely set up with the tools of the trade. In a lecture at the Royal Society of Arts in 1929 he summed up:

> *'I believe I could design, lithograph,*
> *mix the inks necessary, do the printing*
> *and plaster the hoardings with posters, if someone*
> *will pay the perfectly enormous fee I would ask…'*

After WWI Purvis earned his keep both with advertising commissions and with illustrations for magazines such as *Pan* and *John Bull*, and newspapers such as the *Daily Herald* and *The People*. Much of this type of work was carried out for Odham's Press, with whom Purvis would continue to be associated for much of his career. Although a good deal of his early work was therefore in black and white, one cover, for *The London*, was produced in colour, and suggests that Purvis was already experimenting with what was to become his characteristic 'handwriting'.

In 1926 Austin Reed opened his flagship shop in Regent Street and appointed Donald McCullough as his advertising manager. For the launch of the store McCullough developed a co-ordinated campaign with the advertising agents Pritchard Wood. Although a number of different artists were used in its future campaigns, such as McKnight Kauffer and Fougasse, it was Purvis who was to purvey the stylish debonair images of 'The Modern Man' that were to become associated in the public's mind with the store's quality clothing. He had previously done some work for Aquascutum, the sporting and military tailors, where it was

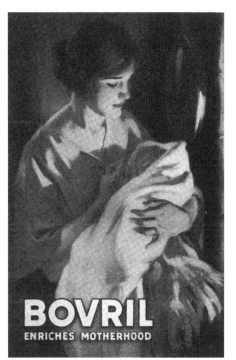

Tom Purvis, showcard for Bovril, 1924

reported that 'a particularly important point has been the rapid increase of postal inquiries since Tom Purvis was commissioned'.

Purvis's Austin Reed men, presented in simple blocks of colour without any detailing or facial features, instantly suggested sophistication, a casual ease and superiority. That attracted buyers, who perhaps hoped that they themselves could acquire such traits merely by buying the clothes. McCullough claimed, in an article in *Commercial Art* in 1929, that Purvis not only had provided most of the illustrations for Austin Reed's advertising and publicity to that date, but had thought up most of the ideas for them as well. He summed up what he considered Purvis's contribution:

'In whatever class of art work is being used it is the Austin Reed policy only to use the best obtainable. Probably the height of superb simplicity in modern men's wear art work is attained by Tom Purvis. These are true, simple, arresting and charming.'

Purvis's style for his work with the railway companies was much the same as that he had developed for Austin Reed. From about 1923 until the end of WWII he produced

Tom Purvis, poster for Austin Reed, 1930s

Tom Purvis, poster for LNER, 1932

Tom Purvis, *Bamburgh Castle*, poster for LNER, 1934

over one hundred railway posters, mainly for LNER. As Purvis was blessed with an inspired advertising man in McCullough, he was lucky enough to find another in William Teasdale, who was appointed LNER's Chief Publicity Manager in 1923. Teasdale was prepared to take a gamble with Purvis's dramatic use of colour and minimal detail, so very different from the studies of historic sites and rural landscapes typical of much railway poster design in the inter-war years. Purvis claimed he was the first artist for the railways to have got away with featureless faces. A baby lying on its back with a rattle, or two 'flappers' chatting, with barely a pier or

ruin in sight, must have been a challenge to the railway boards and shareholders, as well as to many of the general public. In 1925, when Teasdale chose his five 'elite' artists to be under exclusive contract, Purvis was one of the number. It might be partisan to argue that he exerted some influence over his colleagues, but a comparison of Fred Taylor's 'Whitby' of 1928, with a fully rigged ship in port, and his altogether more spare 'Bridlington' of 1935 shows a dramatic leap in the direction of the Purvisesque.

Purvis was to become one of Teasdale's favourites, and was to work equally closely with Teasdale's successor, Cecil Dandridge.

Tom Purvis, poster for LNER, late 1930s

It was Purvis, as one of LNER's contracted artists, who was chosen for the line's 16-sheet posters, designed for street hoardings rather than stations. Purvis is said to have had a great deal of fun preparing for his railway commissions, touring the various routes in his Lancia, sometimes accompanied by his friend and fellow commercial artist Hans Schleger.

Parallel to his work for Austin Reed and LNER, Purvis was producing both posters and press advertisements for many other commercial clients – over sixty throughout his career. Both Shell and BP gave him a variety of commissions during the 1920s and 1930s for posters and lorry bills, for which he would again resort to his flat areas of undelineated colour, but would occasionally include some relevant detail as with car seats, lights and number plates, and even the occasional facial features showing motorists' delight at using such effective petrol. Hewitt suggests that, although Purvis had developed, and largely kept to, his Austin Reed/LNER version of modernism, he did revert to more detailed imagery when this was required, particularly for press advertisements, as he had done in his early work for Aquascutum and Beecham's Pills, when he had had to make greater compromises with copywriters and layout artists.

In spite of his prolific output, Purvis found time to make some contribution to raising the status of his profession, becoming a committee member of the British Society of Poster Designers in 1932, and an early member of the Society of Industrial Artists, being its Vice-President in the latter part of the 1930s. He also fed back into the profession his own ideas on his art with his book *Poster Progress*, published in 1939. The then President of the Art

Tom Purvis, advertisements for Aquascutum Coats, 1924

Tom Purvis, drawings for advertisements for Aquascutum

Directors' Club of New York declared this 'one of the best treatises on poster art I have ever read'; whilst the *British Printer* considered it as 'contributing greatly to the progress of poster art'. Purvis was also active in supporting young talent, judging the Royal Society of Arts competition in design, and being a Visiting Director of Studies to the Commercial Art Department of the Glasgow School of Art. His contribution to design was recognised by his being one of the first group of Royal Designers for Industry, appointed in 1936, and a Fellow of the Faculty in 1939.

During WWII Purvis did some poster work for the Ministry of Information, the Ministry of Supply and the National Savings Committee, but his health was failing and in the post-war years his only major project was the continuation of his work, which had started in the 1930s, for the Blackpool Pleasure Beach Company. Joseph Emberton the architect, who had worked for Austin Reed, was carrying out commissions for the Pleasure Beach and specifically asked for Purvis to work on its advertising and publicity. Along with this work Purvis also designed the Pleasure Beach's mascot, Sunshine Jack.

Although Purvis was perhaps overshadowed by the more experimental modernist McKnight Kauffer in the inter-war years, and was, in the post-war ones, quickly eclipsed by the vibrant originality of the likes of Abram Games, Tom Eckersley, Hans Schleger and F.H.K. Henrion, he was nevertheless one of the most prolific and easily recognised poster designers of his time. His forthright, businesslike approach made him attractive to clients and agencies, his technical know-how provided him with a solid reputation when it came to printers, and the upbeat, colourful simplicity of his style endeared him to the general public.

In speaking of his work Purvis took pride in what he truly believed he had contributed both to the wealth of the country and the aesthetic pleasure of its people. He had little time for those he referred to as 'arty folk', and despised the artist who resorted to advertising work merely to earn money. In an address to the Federation of Master Printers in 1931, he urged printers not only to improve the appearance of their work but to take pride in being true craftsmen rather than tradespeople or even hucksters, and to learn more about what artists were all about [as artists should, in their turn, understand printers]. He declared that he was 'unashamed' to stand up and be counted as a commercial artist:

> *'I am a Commercial Artist and commercial art*
> *demands exactly the same skill, training, knowledge*
> *– genius, if you like – as the Royal Academicians,*
> *with this great difference, that all this skill and effort*
> *must necessarily be subordinated to salesmanship…I*
> *am proud of being a commercial artist, because I*
> *believe that I serve a definite and useful purpose in*
> *life as well as, in a small way, a decorative and, to*
> *some extent, perhaps an inspirational one as well.'*

Tom Purvis, advertisement for Canadian Pacific, 1937

Tom Purvis at work, supported by his beloved Lancia

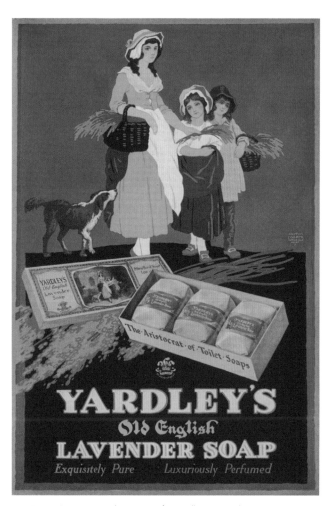

Austin Cooper's 'modern' poster for Yardley's Lavender Soap, 1923

AUSTIN COOPER [1890–1964]

Victoria & Albert Museum website describes Cooper as one of the 'big five' of the 1920s and 1930s when it came to poster design; so one has to ask why he is not better known, and written about, by commentators on, and historians of, commercial art. One possible reason for this may have lain in his own personality, for he was anything but a self-publicist, being rather reserved, serious-looking, and modest. Allied to this is the fact that he was a slightly late developer, and certainly an early retirer, from the scene – his solid working years in graphic design were little more than twenty.

Austin Cooper was a Canadian, born in Manitoba. His family came to Ireland when he was quite young, and later moved on to Wales. He himself moved around a good deal, for once he had finished his art course in Scotland, at the Allan-Fraser Art College, in 1910, he taught for a while in London and, between then and his return to London in 1922, worked back in Canada, and later in New York, making a living as well as he could – as an estate agent, an interior designer of shops and pubs, and an itinerant sign writer.

The first sign that he was putting down roots was when he set up a studio in Montreal with a friend from his college days, Adam Scott, but the partnership was brought to an abrupt end by war service. Cooper was back in England by 1922, working as a freelance artist. An early advertisement he did for Yardley suggests it took him some time to work out a personal style. *Commercial Art* suggested, in a critical comment in 1923, that he was on his way:

'The Cries of London by Wheatley have been the enjoyment of several generations and are still as popular as ever. Messrs. Yardley were therefore well-advised in reviving one of the series for advertising Lavender Soap. By entrusting the task of modernizing the subject to Mr. Austin Cooper they have selected one of the few men who could do justice to their requirements.'

In fact it is hard to discern any signs of modernisation in Cooper's Yardley advertisement, but by the mid-1920s he had adopted the simplicity, bright colours and limited detail of modernism, particularly in his work for London Transport. In 1931 he produced one of his most iconic posters, advertising an exhibition of posters being shown at the Victoria & Albert Museum. And two years later, he produced an even more progressive image for the British Industry Art in the Home Exhibition at the Dorland Hall, in Lower Regent Street, with just the initials BIA dominating the poster. One commentator on this linked Cooper's style to Moholy-Nagy's emphasis on the use of primary shapes, but this could well have been more a matter of zeitgeist than direct influence.

In all, Cooper was to design some fifty posters for London Transport, and he also had commissions from the railways, particularly from LNER and Southern Rail, but from Indian Railways as well. Other organisations for which he provided work included the Empire Marketing Board and the Post Office,

Austin Cooper, self-advertisement, 1923

Austin Cooper, an early advertisement for Eno's Fruit Salts, 1925

Austin Cooper, poster for the Empire Marketing Board, 1920s

Austin Cooper, poster for the GPO, 1930s

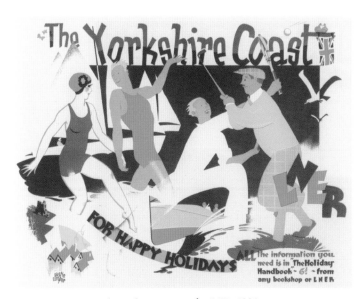

Austin Cooper, poster for LNER, 1930

and a whole variety of companies with products ranging from wirelesses and motor cars, to chocolates and gloves.

There seems to be no record as to why, in 1936, Cooper was chosen, from the brilliant pool of graphic designers in the inter-war years, to be Principal of the Reimann School of Commercial and Industrial Art when it relocated to London from its native Berlin, which it had been forced to do as it was Jewish-owned. Cooper was to run the school through to its closure in 1940 at the commencement of WWII. He gathered round him what Yasuko Suga, in her comprehensive account of the school,

described as 'part-time teaching staff representing what is best and most vital in a very varied field'. The 'field' included display, fashion, dressmaking, photography and interior design, in addition to graphic design – a remarkable range of subjects not to be found together in British colleges at the time.

The Reimann School had begun to exert an influence on British design, particularly display, long before its arrival in London, and on its arrival the more timid commentators saw it as being altogether too 'modern' for the English market. But Cooper defended his school by stressing the eclectic nature of its subjects and teaching

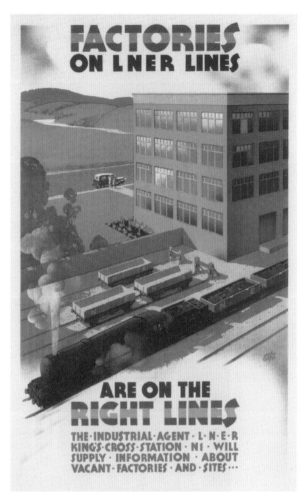

Austin Cooper, poster for LNER, c.1930

styles, and the practical down-to-earth character of its studio system by which students could work on commissions whilst still learning on their courses. Cooper had strong ideas on design education and was an early proposer of a 'centre of excellence', the nub of an idea that lay behind what was eventually to translate into The Design Centre, established post-WWII. In his teaching Cooper was as concerned about the intellectual element to graphic design as he was about its aesthetic and technical aspects. He wrote on this in his description of the Reimann School that appeared in *Art & Industry* in 1939:

> *'The mental approach to one's job is just as important as any other. In order to deal successfully with the wide variety of subjects normally encountered in poster work, it is important that the designer should be well-informed, quick to absorb general and detailed knowledge from the people he meets, the books he reads and – if he is to be abreast of the times, as he should be, from good newspapers and journals – the cultivation of a lively interest in a multitude of things will be of material assistance in providing facts and ideas, the basic content of a poster.'*

Cooper put similar advice into his book *Making a Poster*, which had been published in the previous year by The Studio Ltd. He prefaced this work with a quote from Herbert Read: 'All art depends on the willing devotion of the faculties to an arduous duty.' Cooper gives a brief history of his subject and then takes the reader through the various stages of poster design, providing, generously, illustrations mainly of other designers' work. Although only a short book, covering well-trodden ground, it ends with a totally original and altogether charming admonishment:

'I do not understand why, but almost without exception, students make a habit of parceling their work in such a way as to make necessary unraveling knots impossible…Nothing can be more annoying to the busy business man awaiting sight of the design you have brought to him, than to be kept waiting while you struggle with these ridiculous knots. Please make a point of arranging portfolio or brown paper parcel so that when you are at length ushered into the prescence you can, without any loss of time whatsoever, produce your work.'

Two of the last posters Cooper designed in England, dramatic in red and black, were for the Post Office Savings Bank, linking saving to wartime production needs, and for the Ministry of Information, possibly for a touring exhibition entitled 'How to Fight the Fire Bomb', designed about 1943. From then on Cooper turned from commercial art to becoming a full-time painter. Although this may have been an emotional decision, made on reaching middle age, and may have given him much pleasure, it took him out of the public eye and below its radar; he returned to Canada where he died in 1964.

Austin Cooper, poster for Vitagraph's *Larry Semon*, 1922

85

Anna Zinkeisen, *The Wool Race*, oil on canvas

DORIS CLARE [1898–1991] AND
ANNA KATRINA [1901–1976] ZINKEISEN

he Zinkeisen sisters tend to be rated as merely 'Society' artists, portraitists of the great and the good, decorators of the opulent *Queen Mary*. The only book that attempts to cover their lives and work covers that of their children as well, and gives a relatively brief account of their advertising and publicity work for the press and for posters. Yet the sisters, whose careers sometimes ran together, sometimes veered apart independently, were serious professional artists, unashamed of their commercial work. Anna wrote of such commissions:

> *'You can't set aside your great ambition and your dreams of pure art because you work in an economic and competitive world as well. The idea that the two are incompatible is all wrong.'*

The sisters were from a comfortable middle-class family, initially educated by governesses at home in Scotland. When the family moved down to Pinner in 1909, they continued with what had become an early obsession – to draw and paint – to the near exclusion of applying themselves to other learning. In time they attended art classes at the nearest art school in Harrow, before both won scholarships to the Royal Academy Schools. From the start they were girls who knew their own minds, were confident

Doris Zinkeisen, *"Yoicks!"*, theatre poster, 1925

Anna Zinkeisen, tubecard poster for London Transport, 1934

Anna Zinkeisen, tubecard poster for London Transport, 1934

in their talents, and consequently nearly always determined what commissions they would take and how they would go about them.

Doris, the elder, who had the additional talent of being a skilled horse-rider of competitive national standard, began to interest herself in design for the theatre and films, for which she supplied not only posters but sets and costumes, many of her commissions being for the shows put on by C.B. Cochran.

Both sisters produced posters for transport – Anna some twenty or so for London Transport, with Doris doing the odd one, related to theatre-going; and both worked for LNER, in

this case Doris supplying rather more posters than Anna. In *Art for All* Teri Edelstein describes Anna's London Transport posters as having 'a lively dynamic force', and as 'expressing spontaneity and freedom'. Particularly 'lively' are her 'Motor Show at Olympia', 'Rugby League Cup Final', 'Motor Cycle and Cycle Show at Olympia' and 'RAF Display' – all 'masculine' subjects not normally given to women artists, who were usually allocated flowers or children – and she tackled them with an extraordinary confidence and flair.

In contrast the sisters' posters for LNER are rather staid.

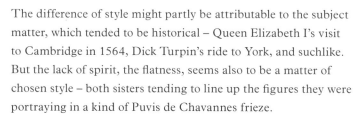

Doris Zinkeisen, poster for LNER, 1930

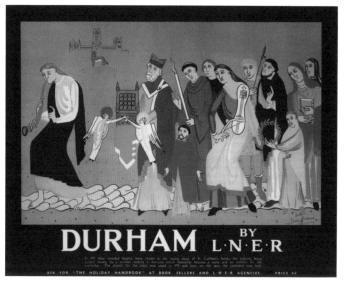

Doris Zinkeisen, poster for LNER, 1932

The difference of style might partly be attributable to the subject matter, which tended to be historical – Queen Elizabeth I's visit to Cambridge in 1564, Dick Turpin's ride to York, and suchlike. But the lack of spirit, the flatness, seems also to be a matter of chosen style – both sisters tending to line up the figures they were portraying in a kind of Puvis de Chavannes frieze.

This ability to produce entirely different styles for different commissions shows itself again in their work for industrial companies. For these, when they were asked for portraits they would be much the same as those done for their private clients, as when each sister contributed to the ICI series 'Portraits of an Industry', which were used in magazine and newspaper advertising from 1944 to 1946. Anna portrayed a chemical engineer and Doris a research chemist. Both retreated to their historical style for United Steel's 'Trade Wind' series, and Anna produced a further Puvis de Chavannes line-up of muscular young men for its 'New Horizon' series. One can hardly believe that the same hands could provide such contrasting images to these series as Doris's surrealistic fantasy to celebrate ICI's introduction of its paint colour monastral blue

Anna Zinkeisen, illustration for United Steel, 1946

advertisements for Charnaux underwear, and, of course, both sisters demonstrated their light-heartedness in their murals for the *Queen Mary* – Anna with her four seasons for the ballroom, and Doris with her 30 ft long 'Entertainment' for the Verandah Grill.

During WWII, when both sisters were auxiliary nurses with the St John Ambulance Brigade, nursing in the morning and painting in the afternoon in a disused operating theatre in St Mary's Hospital, Paddington, the sisters showed yet further versatility both in subject matter and style. Anna made pathological studies of patients for medical research; and Doris, following the liberating army across Europe, provided chilling reportage of Belsen. The sisters did little commercial work after the war, returning to portraiture, Anna rather more than Doris.

Phillip Kelleway, their biographer, is rather dismissive of the sisters' work for advertising and publicity:

> '*The advertiser's art is difficult to say a great deal about; it was commissioned to do a specific task at a given moment. It has not endured in the same way as the portraits have, although it is often ingenious.*'

Yet not a book on railway or underground posters, and there are shelves full, fails to include both Doris's and Anna's images, not infrequently with a text reference [a rarity for a woman poster artist]. And in 1940 Anna's contribution to the Arts was recognised by her being made a Royal Designer for Industry, for her commercial work, an honour given to only three women before her.

in the mid-1930s, or Anna's colourful collage-like image for yet another United Steel series – 'This Present Age'.

And a further twist is Doris's capacity to introduce humour, of a social commentary kind, in her busy press advertisements for Johnnie Walker Whisky Distillers; even stretching to a degree of sauciness in her poster for one of the Cochran shows *On with the Dance* – which the Church Army saw as an 'incentive to prostitution' but Doris considered merely 'frolicsome'. Anna also resorted to cheekiness in her

Doris (left) and Anna (right) Zinkeisen, shown decorating the Grill and Ballroom of RMS Queen Mary, 1935

James Fitton, poster for Ealing Studios, 1949

JAMES FITTON [1899–1982]

ames Fitton was one of the rare examples of an artist who, with politically active working-class roots, and himself an activist, carved out a successful career as a commercial artist. Presumably he was able to accommodate what others might see as a moral conflict between his beliefs and how he chose to earn a living. He was not only to progress up the commercial route to become Art Director for an advertising agency, but to work for that agency for some fifty years.

Fitton was born in Oldham, Lancashire, the son of a trade union leader and a committed Fabian. Like a number of other artists, including Barnett Freedman, an illness [in Fitton's case a bungled operation that left him partially deaf] meant he was off school for some time. Generally rated as useless in most subjects except art, his recuperation would have given him the opportunity to develop his artistic talents as he would.

On leaving school, aged fourteen, he stayed in his home area for some six years, taking on several routine jobs, first with a fabric designer, and then on a newspaper. Nevertheless he maintained his interest in art, attending evening classes at the Manchester School of Art under Adolphe Valette, an artist of some talent himself, albeit nowadays largely remembered as Lowry's teacher.

Fitton came down to London after the end of WWI, the dates variously given as 1919 or 1921. There he got a job with the printer J.S. Riddell, where he stayed for about a year and a half,

amongst other work providing illustrations for 'adventure' subjects for a magazine. As in Manchester, he supplemented what he was learning 'on the job' with evening classes at the Central School of Arts & Crafts under H.S. Hartrick. It was around 1928 that he joined the advertising agency C. Vernon & Sons, where he was to remain for the rest of his career.

C. Harold Vernon, who had founded his agency in about 1885, was a figure of considerable importance in the advertising world – a key player in organising the International Advertising Convention at Wembley in 1924, and President of District 14 [Great Britain] of the Association of Advertising Clubs of the World. Unlike the more ebullient personalities William Crawford and Charles Higham, Vernon has been reported as exerting his influence quietly, working behind the scenes. By the time Fitton joined Vernon's, it was a very well established concern with its own printing works and art department. Vernon fully appreciated the value of the artist to advertising:

'I believe that the future of the Advertising profession is full of promise, provided that Advertising agents allow, and are permitted to allow, their copywriters and commercial artists to develop their allied arts to the full.'

Vernon's own aesthetic sensibilities have been characterised by his having, in his room, a Holbein print over the fireplace and an American poster on another wall. Unlike some other advertising men, Vernon preferred to have his artists with all-round rather than

James Fitton, poster for London Transport, 1937

specialist skills – to be able to design the complete layout including the typography – for which Fitton's time at a printers would have stood him in good stead. And Vernon understood, early on, that the camera would come to predominate in advertising, and that the artist would need to bring more to a project than sound realistic draughtsmanship if he were to survive.

Fitton soon was making his mark at Vernon's and *Commercial Art* was giving him some exposure, using as illustration what it described as 'modernist non-realistic' designs for labels, showcards, poster stamps and a booklet cover. An article on Fitton stressed the humorous side of his work, and described him as having 'a true sense of design'. One of the illustrations is for a label for the agency itself, which was adopted as its trademark.

Fitton's first recorded works were for the Empire Marketing Board and London Tramways. His talent was sufficiently distinguished for Frank Pick, seeing some of Fitton's 'fine art' at the Leicester Galleries in the late twenties, to have recognised his potential for commercial assignments. And, some thirty years later, another talent scout, Sidney John Woods of Ealing Studios, selected Fitton as one of a small band of artists to design film posters – in Fitton's case for *Kind Hearts and Coronets* and *The Galloping Major*. Both Pick and Woods seem to have appreciated what Woods was later to describe as Fitton's 'lightness of touch' – Woods using him for comedies and Pick for places of entertainment, such as the Holborn Empire. And between times Fitton provided advertisements for numerous companies covering a wide range of products and services, including Boots pharmacy,

James Fitton, poster for Romulus Productions, 1951

James Fitton, poster for the Ministry of Food, 1940s

James Fitton, poster for the Ministry of Food, 1940s

James Fitton, poster for ROP, 1940s

Lagonda cars, Mullards wirelesses, and Cornhill Insurance.

But he seems to have had the energy and conviction to lead other parallel lives – that of a 'fine' artist and that of an artist-activist. He was a member of the London Group and the Senefelder Club, and these were not lightweight commitments, for in 1944 he was made an Associate Royal Academician and in 1954 a Royal Academician. In the 1930s his political activities took up a certain amount of his time too. In 1933 he was teaching lithography at the Central School, his students including Pearl Binder, James Holland and Edward Ardizzone, in classes that became a kind of political talking club interspersed with some art. Fitton treated them as colleagues – 'They all knew as much about lithography as I did and they were all as good artists as I was, even better.' One evening, after class, Fitton and some of his students went to Misha Black's studio to hear Clifford Rowe report on his recent visit to the USSR. Out of this meeting grew the Artists' International Association [AIA] aiming to fight Fascism and to democratise art. So whilst Fitton was providing commercial art at Vernon's Studio, he was drawing political cartoons for the *Left Review*! Morris and Radford's stirring account of AIA includes a photograph of Fitton, alongside Ruskin Spear and John Minton, still described as a member of AIA in 1953, some twenty years after the founding of the organisation.

A Royal Academician, a political activist *and* a successful commercial Art Director; Fitton is remembered, in his commercial work, for 'his gift of humorous draughtsmanship' and 'his ability to make his designs tell'; he had joined a thriving agency and had added to its reputation by his own long commitment.

Francis Marshall, 'Only the brave deserve the fair and the fair deserve Jaeger', advertisment for Jaeger, 1940s

FRANCIS MARSHALL [1901–1980]

I n 1934 *Commercial Art* stated that it was only recently that 'artists of any real creative ability have devoted their time and talent to fashion illustration'. And even then it considered that artists that illustrated fashion editorials and features produced altogether finer work than those merely illustrating advertisements. Francis Marshall was one of the few fashion artists who built up a reputation for both editorial and advertising illustration.

As with other types of commercial art, fashion illustration was to have to continually defend itself as a valid outlet for artistic talent. As late as 1951, Audrey Withers, some twenty years the Editor of *Vogue*, protested in the *Penrose Annual*:

> *'What is fashion drawing but a drawing of a well-dressed instead of an undressed woman? What is a drawing for a beauty page but a life drawing of a beautiful head or leg or torso?'*

Fashion artists working for advertising had their own particular challenges – how to produce work that would blend in with copy and typography, how to make an image attractive wherever it was placed on a page, possibly not determined well in advance of publication, and so on.

Francis Marshall was something of a late entrant to the profession, for on leaving school he was intent on a naval career.

Born in 1901, he was old enough to see some service in the Royal Navy Volunteer Reserve towards the end of WWI. After the war he moved into the merchant navy, and then, for a short time, worked in an engineering office. But eventually his interest in drawing grew sufficiently for him to break away from matters naval and to seek a career as a freelance artist, yet one without any formal training in his art. He recalled his first commission as having been a menu for a City restaurant – 'a free lunch and a guinea now and then'.

However, interest was taken in Marshall's efforts to establish himself, and he was encouraged to strengthen his position vis-à-vis the market place by underpinning his natural talent with some formal training. His focus on drawing led him to the Slade School of Fine Art, which had a strong reputation for teaching the subject. Drawing was everything to Marshall – he once declared that 'he would go to the scaffold to defend it'. Throughout his life he kept sketchbooks, roaming the streets, noting down anything that caught his eye, finding 'everything is interesting from beer bottles to Wagnerian tenors'.

Marshall always maintained that his first sketchbook was started at the Ritz in London [under cover of a glass of sherry], to be added to in the Ritz in Paris. He would like to catch, say, the way a waiter stood to take an order, or to light a diner's cigarette. Alison Settle, one-time editor of *Vogue*, wrote of Marshall's obsession with drawing:

> *'The tremendous success that Francis Marshall has so deservedly won is due to the notebooks*

*which he consistently fills with details, all
of which will eventually find their use.'*

After having 'learnt to draw' at the Slade, Marshall decided to join the Carlton Studios – 'to learn how to draw for advertising'. There are various accounts of how he came to be taken on by *Vogue*. Alison Settle's version was that she had noticed figures Marshall had added to a car advertisement and had immediately seen his potential for fashion drawing. He became a staff artist for the magazine from 1928, working both in Paris and in London, and, although coming to specialise in fashion, was called upon to do a variety of other subjects as well.

Marshall's development into a freelance fashion artist appears to have overlapped with his ten-year commitment to *Vogue*, for he is recorded as drawing for Jaeger as early as 1934, although his more prolific work for them was in the post-WWII years, with the emphasis on advertising for the expansion of exports. Fashion drawing for exports advertising brought its own challenge as the work had to be completed a considerable time in advance of the fashions actually becoming available. *Vogue* had helped Marshall build a reputation as a fashion illustrator, and Jaeger was to validate him as a fashion artist for advertising. He was to supply drawings for all Jaeger departments, from knitwear to accessories, and is credited with devising its three-line 'straw' logo that was to appear on all its post-war packaging and publicity.

During the war Marshall worked in Admiralty camouflage with official leave to provide sketches of members of the armed forces and of munitions workers for the Ministry of Information, and drawings for the Ministry of Transport. Returning to fashion drawing at the end of the war, he built up an impressive list of clients, accepting advertising assignments for a number of companies unrelated to fashion, such as Boots pharmacy and the Westminster Bank, and even undertaking posters for films.

But fashion is where his legacy lies and, in addition to Jaeger, his most memorable images are for Tootal Broadhurst and Elizabeth Arden. *Art & Industry* in 1952 wrote of the Elizabeth Arden advertisements:

> *'With a beautifully designed product to start with,
> a first rate fashion artist like Francis Marshall
> and copy writers who understood the meaning
> of brevity and kept to the point, the advertising
> was immediately in character with the product
> to be sold and resulted in considerable market
> expansion which has increased since the war.'*

With Tootal, Marshall had the task of providing illustrations to sell fabrics, which meant that he might only receive a tentative sketch of the material from which he would have to envisage its adaptability for different garments. One of his most notable series – 'All the World Over' – was part of another campaign to further exports.

Although Marshall's drawings would often give the impression of having been done swiftly, usually many sketches would have preceded the final version, done with a carbon pencil and Indian ink, sometimes with coloured washes. The end result could well give a feeling of haste, belying the effort behind it, but this could also be interpreted as 'haste' to get 'the latest thing' quickly to the market. Marshall was in constant demand at this time and much lauded. Madge Garland, a fan and one-time fashion editor at *Vogue*, rated him as the most notable contemporary fashion artist, and wrote of his drawings that they 'bewitched feminine hearts and lightened masculine pockets'.

Marshall wrote books on both fashion drawing and magazine illustration, generously using other artists' work along with his own to exemplify his teaching points. He wrote simply and sensibly, demonstrating his own enthusiasm for, and satisfaction with, his chosen career, and recommending it to others:

'It is one of the best paid branches of commercial art and one of the most interesting, concerning as it does every phase of modern life. A true fashion artist has a grandstand view of the world.'

Francis Marshall, advertisment for Elizabeth Arden, 1940s

PROGRAM

... in the program are special events in:

Opening Cere...

H. M. The King will decla...
of Britain open after a S...
St. Paul's Cathedral...

EXHIBITI...

LONDO...
May 4—Septer...
South Bank Ex...
May 3—Oct...
Festival Pleasure Garde...
May 3—Sept...
Exhibition of...
South Kens...
Exhibition of A...
Lansbury,...
Exhibition...
Victoria and Al...

GLAS...
May 28—...
Exhibition of Industri...

BEL...
June 1—...
Ulster Farm and...

ARTS F...
There will be a Spec...
Arts in LOND...
Aberdeen Festival...

eric fraser

FESTIVAL OF BRITAIN

1851   1951

MAY 3—SEPTEMBER 30, 1951

Eric Fraser, *Locomotion*, headpiece for Barker's of Kensington, 1925

ERIC FRASER [1902–1983]

Eric Fraser is best remembered as an illustrator, particularly for the *Radio Times*, a magazine that was to be found in most homes of wireless owners throughout the 20th century. Books and articles on Fraser make some mention of his commercial work, supplying an odd image here and there, and perhaps the odd sentence with a bunched-up list of some of the companies commissioning him, but usually this is subordinated to his work as an illustrator.

A typical evaluation of Fraser's commercial output is given by Alec Davies:

'Eric Fraser has achieved his standard despite the quantity of his drawings, despite the need to appeal to large groups of people who cannot necessarily be assumed to have a highly developed aesthetic sense; despite the limited objective of story illustration and the still closer limitation of advertisement illustration, where the advertiser's aim is commercial and only indirectly concerned with artist merit.'

What grudging snobbery – despite selling himself and his talents, he didn't do too badly! Fraser's agent, R.P. Gossop, gives an altogether more positive version of Fraser's 'selling out':

'…he has made a deliberate choice and he has not merely wandered in with a vague feeling that this is as good as any other means of turning his years of training and the hard labour of life school to account …'

Fraser's 'training' and 'hard labour' took place in London; he was born in Westminster in 1902. He showed early artistic ability, and even while he was still at secondary school

Eric Fraser, 'program' of events for the American market, Festival of Britain, 1951

Eric Fraser, line illustrations, 1925

he attended classes at Westminster College of Art under Walter Sickert. With the encouragement of his art master he achieved a scholarship to Goldsmiths' College of Art, where he studied in the graphics department from 1919 to 1924 under Edmund Sullivan, himself a commercial artist of some repute. Fraser received his first commission whilst still an art student – a Christmas catalogue illustration for Barker's of Kensington.

Fraser was later to teach at Camberwell School of Art [through to 1940] and, for a short time, at the Reimann School when it relocated from Germany in the 1930s. But alongside this Fraser was building up his remarkable career as an illustrator and advertising artist, working from various studios in London until 1938, and from then onwards from his homes in Twickenham and then Hampton.

Fraser's first commission for the *Radio Times* was in 1926, and interspersed with his regular contributions to that magazine he was to provide work for over thirty other concerns, public and private, from heavy industry to beer, from railways to finance to films. In 1991 British Gas sponsored a touring exhibition – *Eric Fraser: An Illustrator of Our Time*. Although it had been the wont of a few commercial organisations to sponsor shows of commercial artists, these were invariably of the works done for their own advertising and publicity, Shell and LNER for example. That British Gas was willing to mount an exhibition of the total range of one of their commissioned artists was not only further publicity for themselves but a matter of gratitude to an artist who had done so much for the reputation of the gas industry as a whole. Apart from his other work for the industry, Fraser's 'Mr. Therm' was the main brand image for the Gas, Light & Coke Company for some thirty years, and had no doubt brought the company good returns.

It was in 1931 that the Public Relations Department of the Company commissioned Fraser to provide them with a 'character' that they could use in their advertising, based on the properties and look of a flame of gas. The Company's previous 'Spirit of Coal'. Designed by Septimus Scott and used in the British Empire Exhibition in 1924, had failed to catch the public's imagination. Anne Clendinning in *Demons of Domesticity* described the initial impact of Mr. Therm:

> *'Within months of his first appearance, Mr. Therm's flat schematic face, haloed head, and stylized limbs appeared on hoardings, buses, trade exhibition posters and in showroom windows.'*

Mr. Therm was to prance his way, ever smiling, not only on posters and in press advertisements, but in a myriad of other forms – on De La Rue playing cards, on the sides of toy cars, as tin badges besported by children, in cookery books such as *Mr. Therm goes Country*, and so on. In fact, Mr. Therm became a kind of domestic consultant – helping consumers make the best use of the gas supply coming to them in their cookers, heaters, refrigerators, and even washing machines.

Fraser was to have scathing things to say both about his

Eric Fraser, *Mr. Therm*, poster for the Gas Council, 1940

Eric Fraser, publicity leaflet for Hastings Borough Council, 1947

initial payment for the character – five guineas – and about later appearances of Mr. Therm, rolled out by studio artists at the London Press Exchange [who were themselves later reported to have had a good deal of fun continuing to draw Mr. Therm in his various guises]. Mr. Therm was pensioned off in 1962, with the arrival of North Sea Gas. Colman, Prentis & Varley took over the Company's publicity in that year and found themselves stuck with a creature with 'an annoying wide smile and bright-eyed cheeriness' which they felt no longer symbolised the speed and efficiency of the industry.

Mr. Therm brought a light touch to what could have been a stolid subject, and was altogether more humorous than much of Fraser's other commercial work, which tended to the historical and literary, as with his 'Achilles being dipped in the Styx' for Imperial

Eric Fraser, poster for London Transport, 1928

Chemical Industries. There was only an occasional opportunity to show satirical wit, his spoof of the Bayeux Tapestry for the Borough of Hastings' publicity being one of them. Yet he was perfectly capable of producing strikingly modernist images when these were required, as his London Transport posters for a motor show at Olympia and for a Cup Final demonstrate. Fraser seems to have lived an uncomplicated life, providing his illustrations for the BBC and for publishers along with his commercial assignments, working within budgets to very tight schedules, mainly using pen, poster paint or watercolour. And, as Gossop his agent wrote, this was his chosen way of using his talents; he is said never to have done a drawing just for wanting to draw, without a commission, deriving thereby not only a good income but much enjoyment, from being an unashamed artist.

Tom Eckersley and Eric Lombers, tubecard poster for London Transport, 1935

TOM ECKERSLEY [1914–1997]

Tom Eckersley was born in Manchester. Like a few other commercial artists, early childhood illness provided him with the time for what Paul Rennie, his archivist, referred to as 'occupational therapy', drawing and painting during his absences from school. Eckersley himself, in his book *Poster Designs*, wrote that he knew from an early age that he wanted to be a commercial artist, and that from the first it was posters that attracted him. He not only became a distinguished commercial artist, amongst the top dozen in the country, but was also to be a pioneer educationalist in the field of graphic design.

Eckersley trained at the Salford School of Art, where his natural talent was soon recognised; he was awarded the Hayward medal as best student. It was whilst he was at Salford that he met up with Eric Lombers, a fellow student, and on the completion of their course the pair came down to London, intent on finding commissions as commercial artists. An introduction to Frank Pick, from one of their tutors, proved to be the start of Eckersley's long association with London Transport. It was to last through to his retirement, some fifty years in all, during which he produced more than eighty designs for them. Eckersley and Lombers were young enthusiasts, proactive in selling their talents, and, along with London Transport commissions, they showed that they were prepared to turn their hands to anything that presented itself – illustrations

Tom Eckersley, poster for London Transport, 1954

Tom Eckersley, poster for the RoSPA, 1940s

for the *News Chronicle*, a shop window for Permutit, and part-time teaching at the Westminster College of Art.

By the onset of WWII the partnership had virtually broken up, Eckersley going into the RAF and Lombers into the army. Eckersley started work as a cartographer but was transferred to the Publicity Section of the Air Ministry, which enabled him to carry on with some freelance work as well. It was during the war that he developed his work for the Post Office, and began his prolific publicity work with the Royal Society for the Prevention of Accidents [RoSPA]. Rennie records Lombers and Eckersley submitting work to the Post Office soon after their arrival in London in 1934, but it was during the war that Eckersley built on the relationship that was to last well into the post-war years. With the Post Office commissions he found scope for humour, particularly memorable being his variations on the theme 'Please Pack Parcels Very Carefully'.

Eckersley became the main designer of RoSPA posters during the war, producing some two dozen for munitions workers, industrial accidents having risen considerably with the intake of women and novices to replace the men now in the services. His RoSPA work clearly illustrates his stylistic preference for one key dominating feature – a hammer, a ladder, a body falling – with minimal copy, the image largely telling the story. Mary Gowing protested that Eckersley's preference for the image to express the intended emotion 'made copywriters weep', albeit she appreciated that it was his skill in expressing emotion that led to his success as a poster designer:

'Tom Eckersley's propaganda flies, as the crow flies, by the shortest route to the heart and the head of the ordinary man. By the most ruthless scrapping of the non-essential, by the perfect mating of chosen word with chosen picture, he wings the total message.'

Eckersley provided press advertisements and posters for dozens of companies from airlines [BEA, Aer Lingus and Pakistan International] to films [Ealing Studios]; from industry [British Aluminium] to clothing [Austin Reed and Tootal Ties]. Perhaps his two best-remembered campaigns were for Gillette razors and Eno's Fruit Salts.

The catchwords 'Good mornings begin with Gillette' had initially been illustrated by David Langdon. When Eckersley came to do the illustrations he paired happy [without a beard] with unhappy [bewhiskered] animals – goats, seals, poodles etc. – and nationalities – Mexicans, Egyptians, Scots etc. – all in striking colours. The campaign was handled by W.S. Crawford's advertising agency, as was the Eno's campaign. In his book *Poster Design* Eckersley provides the reader with a rare insight into how he developed his ideas for advertising fruit salts, over time and through discussions with Ashley Havinden, Crawford's Art Director, who had briefed him with the word 'cheerfulness'. The images morphed from a man's smiling face behind a glass of bubbles, through a profile with a hand holding a glass of bubbles, to a final version – a spoon, whose handle was a smiling man's face, in a glass of bubbles, the predominant colour being blue, emotive of cool and fresh.

Tom Eckersley, poster for Pakistan International Airlines, c.1960

111

Tom Eckersley, poster and sketches for Eno's Fruit Salt, 1947

Mary Gowing had written in 1947 that, if her advertising colleagues chose to work with the likes of Eckersley, a School of British Advertising might come into being – its techniques studied and its influence respected. Her words foreshadowed Eckersley's actions, for in 1954 he joined the teaching staff of the London College of Printing and proceeded to establish the first British undergraduate course in graphic design, which he was to head for some twenty years, to 1977. With such pupils at the extremes of intent as Ralph Steadman and Charles Saatchi, Eckersley's influence can be rated a very wide one indeed!

His message was that 'unashamed' artists should rightly be so:

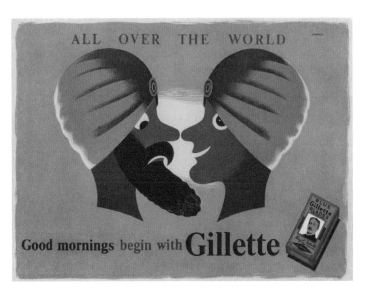

'To me the calibre of a designer lies in his ability to accept …specific limitations and out of them to produce a poster which will first of all do the job required of it, at the same time never compromising his own personal basic principles of design and good taste…'

Eckersley was awarded an OBE in 1948; and in 1977 he was given a retrospective exhibition at the London College of Printing, now a constituent part of the University of the Arts, where his archive is held.

Tom Eckersley, posters for Gillette Razor Blades, 1950s

Stephen Tallents, promotional
portfolio of the firm's work for
Cockade Exhibitions, 1950s
Before becoming a director of
Cockade, Sir Stephen Tallents
worked for the Empire Marketing
Board, the GPO, and the BBC

PATRONS OF 'UNASHAMED' ARTISTS

'…[he] combines a knowing respect for the past in printing with an active appreciation of the most modern in pictorial art. He has had the courage to introduce work which many of his contemporaries regard as extremist and has had the satisfaction of seeing others follow where he has led.'

hese words were written in 1926 of Gerard Meynell, who ran the Westminster Press, and something similar could be written about dozens of entrepreneurs in advertising and publicity, now largely forgotten: *éminences grises* who had the confidence and the perceptiveness to commission often unknown, frequently 'dangerously progressive' artists to further the aims of their organisations. In an *Art & Industry* critique of a Shell-Mex BP exhibition of their posters in 1938, somewhat curiously opened by the poet T.S. Eliot, there is comment on the preferred anonymity of one such patron:

> *'Nowhere in the catalogue, needless to say, does Jack Beddington's name appear. Not as an after-thought, therefore, but in emphasis of his habitual anonymity, is tribute paid last rather than first to the presiding genius of Shell-BP publicity. But to all who matter his name is writ large over this exhibition.'*

In my brief appreciation of Beddington [2006], I entitled him 'the footnote man', occasionally appearing as a footnote in the biographies of others [in Beddington's case, in those of the likes of McKnight Kauffer, John Betjeman and John Piper], but yet to have any comprehensive account of his contribution to others' careers. In the inter-war years there were many such 'footnote' people, who courageously championed artists, frequently having to argue their cases against conservative Boards, and without whose patronage many 'unashamed' artists could not have survived, and indeed flourished, in their chosen calling.

Frank Pick at London Transport and Jack Beddington at Shell-Mex BP are the two patrons of the inter-war years that now most readily come to mind, although even they have yet to have the comprehensive biographies they merit. But who now so much as recognises the name Christian Barman, Pick's architect-trained right-hand man, or Harold Hutchinson, who succeeded Barman and continued the London Transport commitment to modernism? And although there are shelves full of books devoted to the wonderful railway posters of the 1920s and 1930s, who now can name the men, say at LNER, whose energy and enthusiasm fuelled their existence, William Teasdale and his aide and successor Cecil Dandridge?

The list is not an endless one, for it was a period when advertising and publicity were struggling to establish themselves as valid professions and few individuals had the drive of a missionary to spearhead the cause. Further exceptional names were Stephen Tallents at the Empire Marketing Board and the Post Office, and Sidney Rogerson at ICI, both not only championing their artists but having the vision of how art could be harnessed, beyond the boundaries of their own organisations, for governmental propaganda.

And there were those with a lighter touch, a more parochial intent, such as the 'footnote' men of retail – W.D. McCullough, Advertising Manager of Austin Reed, who pushed to place advertising at the heart of his company's policy making, and who appreciated the potential of the artist not only to sell products but to sell an 'image'; J.W. Cassels at Moss Bros. – an early commissioner of such humorists as Bateman and Heath Robinson; Colonel Wyld, who saw advertising as essential for his expansionist ambitions, letting other humorists run wild at Fortnum & Mason; and W. Buchanan-Taylor, Publicity Manager of J. Lyons & Co., who had the challenge of having to advertise an enormous range of products and services – from twopenny cups of tea to banquets for thousands, from Swiss rolls to luxury suites at the Regent Palace Hotel.

These, and other patrons of unashamed artists, such as Colin Anderson of the Orient Line, Sidney John Woods of Ealing Studios, and Douglas Wilson at United Steel, not only

commissioned artists, sometimes providing them with a modest stipend, but wrote, lectured, laid on exhibitions and politicised to raise the status, as well as the standard, of art and design in advertising and publicity. All are awaiting fuller recognition of their contributions.

CHRISTIAN BARMAN

f Christian Barman is remembered at all nowadays, it is likely to be more by railway enthusiasts than by followers of the arts. People interested in inter-war London Transport posters may recall him only as the biographer of Frank Pick, a book that Oliver Green, historian of London Transport, described as 'frustratingly patchy'. There is, however, a promising unpublished thesis on Barman lying in the archives of the Royal Society of Arts [RSA], possibly unpublished because the subject was not considered of sufficient interest to attract a market!

Yet Barman, quite apart from being a patron of unashamed artists, both at London Transport and at the British Transport Commission, was himself a man of no mean talent – architect, industrial designer, typographer, broadcaster, writer and novelist. He was one of only a handful of publicity people to have received an OBE, as well as being elected a Royal Designer for Industry.

That he is not as well known as Pick or Beddington may partly be due to his own personality, for, as his son said of him, 'he was a very modest man, almost to self-effacement'. Enid Marx, who personally volunteered to collect related ephemera for his archive at the RSA, wrote of him:

> '...he was the sort of person, very anonymous, and the interesting thing was he was very anonymous in a very determined way.'

Barman was born in Antwerp in 1898, his father being a captain for the Red Star Line that sailed from that port. In WWI the family settled in England, the father then sailing from English ports. The family, curiously, became naturalised Americans, presumably because it was their intention to live there; Barman did not take British citizenship until 1931.

In 1916 he enrolled in the Architectural School of Liverpool University; in 1919 his family returned to Belgium but he decided to remain in England. It was during his time at university that Barman developed what has been described as his 'civic' sense, a concern for people and their designed environment. He founded and edited *Architecture*, a vehicle for expressing his concerns. From this Barman went on to edit the *Architect's Journal* and to co-edit the *Architectural Review*. Meanwhile he had set up his own design and architectural practice, working on small projects and designing for HMV's Household Appliance Department – a convector heater and iron that were ground breaking in their design at that time.

Barman had, for some time, admired Pick and his pioneering work at London Transport, and Pick was certainly aware of what Barman was doing, for Barman recorded that:

> '*On Thursday, 3rd January, 1935, a letter arrived at my office in Davies street where I carried out a modest practice as architect and designer. It was quite short, only three lines. "Will you come and see me? I would like a few words with you."*'

Pick, by then Chairman of the London Transport Board, offered Barman the newly created post of Publicity Officer; and so commenced the 'partnership', lasting some six years from 1935 to 1941, in which Barman became Pick's 'eyes and ears'. There are few accounts of how the actual relationship worked. Barman records, in his biography of Pick, that he tended to complain that no one stood up to him, and that he would like 'real dialogues' with his colleagues. Barman goes on to write, modestly, 'I was one of the fortunate ones who managed to sustain that kind of relationship.' At the end of Barman's first year he received a note from Pick:

> '*I like your open critical mind. I like your disagreement with me and my old-fashioned notions. I like your bold arguments. I intend to go on struggling with you for my own, and I trust, your profit.*'

In spite of the fact that Pick was now running the whole organisation, he liked to approve everything that was going on, and Barman was prepared to fit in with this, so it is not always easy to tease out his exact contribution to any project or commission. Something of how it worked can be seen from an account, by the young Tom Eckersley, of receiving a commission from Barman:

> *'Barman's secretary would ring up and say Mr.*
> *Barman would like to see you at one o'clock. Or*
> *have tea with you. He would always define the*
> *problem for you at the beginning but would always*
> *consult with Mr. Pick who insisted on seeing all*
> *designs. Barman treated artists exceptionally well.*
> *You didn't get much contact but he rarely turned*
> *things down… You couldn't get away with anything*
> *from Barman, but he really liked my work.'*

What is certain is that Barman championed his artists. In 1936 he wrote an appreciation of Enid Marx in *Signature*, pointing out her skill as a printmaker as well as a textile designer, and applauding the 'fitness and simplicity' of her work. In the same article he expressed the view that commercial artists, taking commissions, need not feel constrained thereby:

> *'But subjects and problems furnished by the*
> *requirements of other people need never fail,*
> *as long as the hand keeps its cunning; and the*
> *mind that is privileged regularly to exercise*
> *itself upon such problems need have little fear*
> *that it may grow prematurely stale.'*

And, yet again, in a short piece on the work of Hans Schleger, in *Art & Industry* in 1937, one can glean some idea of how Barman saw his briefs as not so much limiting creativity as motivating it:

> *'If he has to do a mere drawing he will…do a very creditable*
> *piece of work; confront him with a very nasty situation*
> *in marketing psychology and he will show his genius.'*

It was Barman who persuaded London Transport to accept Schleger's progressive design for a poster for the annual RAF display at Hendon in 1935; and similarly he argued for the employment of the radical Moholy-Nagy, whom Pick considered did no more than produce 'surrealistic pastiche'. Eventually Pick gave way and involved Moholy-Nagy in the design of the British pavilion in the 1937 Paris Exhibition, along with accepting some safety posters from him. And Barman showed an equal determination in getting, in 1936, a Man Ray design – 'London Transport – Keep London Going' – a totally atypical design, the like of which had not been seen before on the underground.

Oliver Green supplies a rare anecdote of when Barman did turn down work. In 1937 Barman had required two posters from Eric Ravilious featuring Greenwich, and his response to what was offered shows something of the firmness of resolve that must have stood him well in his relationship with Pick:

> *'Although I greatly like the drawing I have here, I think*
> *it is completely useless for the purpose of attracting traffic*

*to Greenwich. Kensal Rise with a stiff wind blowing
would be just about equivalent in traffic value.'*

In 1940 Barman wrote a summary article on London
Transport publicity for the *Penrose Annual*. The pronoun 'I' does
not appear once! Yet from the article one can see his understanding
of the challenge that was set its poster artists, especially the
smallness of the size they had to work with – double royal. And
he writes with a sensitive appreciation of Edward Bawden's
experiments with linocuts, of John Farleigh combining woodcuts
with lithography, of Barnett Freedman's use of transparent varnish,
of Beck's use of photography, and of F.H.K. Henrion's experiments
with tinting. Yet again, in this summary, Barman emphasises the
artist's potential satisfaction to be derived from commercial work:

> *'Experiments such as these have proved worthwhile
> in many ways, not least because they have aroused
> a keenness of interest and a sense of adventure
> in artists and printers alike…Such interest as its
> [LT's] advertising possesses is largely due to the
> number and variety of collaborators who have been
> consistently encouraged to give of their best.'*

During WWII Barman was attached to the Directorate of
Works; and at the end of the war he joined Great Western Railways
as its Publicity Adviser. He had hardly got his feet under the table
there when there was the nationalisation of transport and he was
appointed Chief Publicity Officer for the British Transport Board.
Barman was determined to apply to the railways what had been
achieved by London Transport, but it was an uphill climb, for the
Board was absorbed in massive organisational changes and had
little time for the niceties of aesthetics. Nevertheless Barman's
gritty determination led to the establishment of the Railway Design
panel, of which he acted as the executive member. Inevitably, in
this role, Barman became more remote from artists, and more
concerned with organisational effectiveness – 'a pioneer in the
management of design'. Barman's writings also become more
orientated to transport planning and design, yet even well into the
1950s he was still interesting himself in such matters as lettering
and printers' ornamentation.

Barman's obituaries tell of 'a man of short stature and quiet
enthusiasm', modest and unassuming, and many recorded that they
felt his considerable achievements had yet to be fully acknowledged.
The Society of Industrial Artists recorded how many of their
members 'owe him grateful thanks for his patronage in their salad
days'; and, on a personal level, Enid Marx added touchingly:

> *'He will always be affectionately remembered by those
> of us who had the good fortune to work for him.'*

When Barman wrote of Harold Curwen, another patron
of artists, as a quiet, mild-mannered man, whom people did not
appreciate as having an inner core of extreme toughness, he could
well have been describing himself.

WILLIAM TEASDALE AND CECIL DANDRIDGE

In 1931 a contributor to *Commercial Art* wrote of his visit to an LNER Poster Exhibition:

'Why all this fuss about railway posters – theirs is an easy proposition. They have only to use the multitude of interesting and beautiful places on their line and the rest is easy. I wonder what sort of job they would make of advertising cheese… Come to the exhibition with me for an hour and browse around the walls and you will see for yourself that they would make a very good job of advertising cheese or soap or any other commodity for that matter…There is obviously a directing mind behind it all – an astute one. See how he plays on the emotions, using first one string and then another to induce travel on LNER. Perhaps one may be permitted to mention his name – Mr. C. Dandridge, who has played up well to the able lead of his predecessor, Mr.Teasdale, upon whose solid foundations he has had the wit to build and extend.'

 s Frank Pick, Christian Barman and Harold Hutchinson were the *éminences grises* behind London Transport publicity, so William Teasdale and Cecil Dandridge were the spur for the posters of the London, Northern & Eastern Railway [LNER] , generally considered the most committed and progressive of the four merged railway companies as far as 'aesthetic' publicity was concerned.

Teasdale already had relevant experience before taking up his post at LNER, having been Trade Advertising Agent for North Eastern Railway, one of the merged companies. At LNER his task was that much larger – the company controlled railway travel from Essex in the south to Dunbar in the North, with a vast administrative organisation made up of many departments, each of which had to be negotiated with on matters of budget, what to publicise, when, where and how. But Teasdale was well up to the challenge. He was to reign for some half-dozen glorious years, from 1923 to 1929, when he was promoted to become Assistant Manager of the Company. Even in this position he continued to keep his eye on what was going on in the Publicity Department.

Teasdale was to break new ground in several ways. Early on he dispensed with 'bought-in' images whereby firms of printers offered their wares, a custom which could well have fitted the Yorkshire Dales or the Borders. He rarely even took submitted work offered by artists – an exception being two from Tom Purvis, which he bought immediately on sight. Teasdale decided what was wanted, and then chose the artist he thought most suitable to the subject and treatment he had in mind, for example Fred Taylor for an architectural theme, Frank Mason for a marine one. Not only was Teasdale concerned to catch the spirit of a destination, just as he had conceived it, but he had the commercial wit to set up joint projects with resorts, where both his company and the town would profit from such cooperation. One of the earliest such schemes was when Gregory Brown produced a poster for Scarborough. Another example was when York Minster needed to raise restoration funds and Taylor was commissioned to provide what was to become one of his most iconic views.

A further Teasdale innovation was to establish an artist 'superteam'. In 1926 he contracted five artists to produce work solely for LNER of the railway companies, and offered, in return, a guaranteed minimum income, the arrangement to last until 1929. The five artists he chose were Fred Taylor, Frank Newbould, Austin Cooper, Frank Mason and Tom Purvis. They were paid according to Teasdale's evaluation, Taylor getting the highest rate. Teasdale wrote of the relationship:

'These men of temperament quickly appreciated business facts, and I have always found that it pays to treat the artist as if he were a colleague in business; tell him all the essentials and then leave him alone.'

One aspect of Teasdale's 'essentials' was that the artists should familiarise themselves with the destination they were to portray. Taylor, for example, travelled to the continent to fulfil this requirement. After such visits Teasdale trusted his 'team' to get on with the job, albeit he might give the odd nudge when an idea occurred to him. The scheme was extended to 1932, when the company came under financial strain and it was withdrawn. Nevertheless the artists remained loyal to LNER and continued to welcome commissions although they had no legal obligation to do so.

When it came to 'style', Teasdale was not much taken with 'modernism' and, as an article in *Commercial Art* put it:

'…steered that difficult middle course between a mere freakish and denationalized modernity and the obsolete method of applying to the boarding the type of art which had been developed for vastly different uses.'

Teasdale was rated by Shaw Sparrow as 'a man of genius in the world of advertising'; and certainly he can be credited with spearheading a new kind of railway poster that other companies were soon to imitate. He was concerned that LNER should have its own 'image', and this was to include not only image but typography – it should have unified print, whether on advertising, on timetables, for station signs, or for locomotives and other stock. It was Teasdale's assistant Cecil Dandridge who was to carry through Teasdale's ambition.

Although Dandridge was a 'railway man', working on the passenger management side [with wartime spells as traffic officer in Turkey and Russia], he was committed to the use of 'good' art for railway publicity, and, more idealistically, to advance public taste. In 1937 he wrote of his efforts:

'To keep up to date with current ideas in artistic expression as applied to advertising, I make it a practice to visit many Exhibitions, to scan the pages of British and

International publications devoted to painting and design, to encourage, by means of competitions and criticism, the work of Art Schools, and to examine carefully any new work which may have been submitted for consideration.'

It was in Dandridge's time that the LNER annual poster exhibition was moved from King's Cross Station into the West End, to the New Burlington Galleries, perhaps reflecting Dandridge's intent not only to continue Teasdale's concern for good art on the railways, but actually to raise the status of its posters. *Commercial Art* in 1926 included an item on Dandridge's promising start in following in Teasdale's steps:

'Mr. Dandridge has achieved distinguished success in the handling of traffic problems. Like his predecessor he is a railwayman and has a thorough knowledge of railway organization, which, in his present position, is more of an essential requirement than a preoccupation with matters of art. But he shows already that he has the keen discrimination which picks out good design from indifferent. His youthful appearance and pleasant manners do not disguise his practical ability.'

When it came to a standardised type, Dandridge was faced with the problem of legibility – relatively easy with stationery and booklets, but altogether more difficult when the message on a poster needed to be comprehended across a platform or railway lines. Along with the basic criteria of legibility, practicality and economy, Dandridge was concerned with acceptability and with getting a new typeface approved throughout his organisation, as well as by the myriad of printers used by LNER, at one time thought to be about ninety.

Eric Gill had already been experimenting with his typeface Gill Sans, a name given to it by Stanley Morison, who was encouraging Gill with its development. Some work was in hand with London Transport when Dandridge began discussions with Gill about its possible use with LNER. Dandridge described the adaptation of Gill's type for his company's needs:

'LNE Railway Gill Sans is without ornament or serif and represents in any size or weight about the maximum clarity which can be obtained from the printed word.'

In introducing the type Dandridge wrote regular updates in the pages of LNER 'Advertising Notes', keeping staff abreast of progress. Soon Gill Sans was established throughout the company and Dandridge recorded with some pride:

'Its universal use by our printers, architects, artists, signwriters and electrical engineers has already brought about a marked change in the appearance of our printed material, stations, receiving offices, and agencies…it now constitutes what may be regarded as the largest type reformation of our time.'

In 1932, when all the changes had been made, Dandridge got Gill to pose by the Flying Scotsman, for which Gill had hand-painted the front sign. He was rewarded with a ride on the footplate, a long-held ambition. Gill Sans remained the LNER type, and when the railways were nationalised it was used throughout the national network.

SIDNEY ROGERSON [1894 –1968]

In one respect Sidney Rogerson, like Stephen Tallents, towered above other greats of organisational patronage in that he was not only concerned to commission artists to progress the fortunes of his own company, but he envisaged their employment beyond this – to publicise both his industry [chemicals] and, even further, his country. He was a man with vision; possibly something of his father's career as a clergyman had rubbed off, for he was not only a visionary but a missionary.

Sidney Rogerson was the Publicity Controller for Imperial Chemical Industries [ICI] for twenty years, from 1932, when he joined the company, to 1952. All accounts of his early life, and they are sparse, show him to have entered publicity from a military background; and certainly he is better known today by military historians, for his books on his experiences in WWI, than by design historians for his patronage of the arts. However, there is just a hint to be gleaned from an article by Sir Henry Rushbury on industrial patronage [*Art & Industry*, 1950] that Rogerson had an aesthetic element running through his veins from the start:

> *'Himself a sensitive person, who, had it not been for the First World War, might now have been an artist…'*

This suggests that Rogerson's early ambition towards an art education may well have been frustrated by war service. In WWI he was commissioned in the West Yorkshire Regiment, and later he recorded his battleground experiences in two much quoted books – *Twelve Days on the Somme* [1933] and *The Last of the Ebb'* [1937].

There is something of a blank as to what Rogerson did immediately after the war ended, but by 1923 he was working with the Federation of British Industries [FBI] as its Publicity Manager, a post he held until 1930. His appointment may well have been on the unsubstantiated assumption that if you can lead men in battle you can lead them in peace. Nevertheless Rogerson must have proved himself in publicity, for not long after joining ICI, in 1930, he was promoted to the position of Publicity Controller, a term not used by other organisations but one not inappropriate to him, for Rogerson was to hold the reigns tightly in his hands.

Industry had made little use of artists for their publicity up to that time. In 1928 the *Advertiser's Annual* complained that industry gave little thought to how their advertising looked; that technical advertising was usually no more than a piece of machinery along with claims, sometimes vague, as to its unique selling points; that one technical advertisement was indistinguishable from another. And some two years later *Commercial Art* continued along much the same lines:

> '*The word Technology is often used to express
> advertisements which may give brass tacks, but do it so
> awkwardly and clumsily that the effect is repellent. In
> other words technical advertising is amateur advertising.*'

There seems to have been little incentive for industry to improve its advertising and publicity as it was assumed that because it was placed mainly in the technical press, not read by the 'man in the street', all that was required was technical information, aesthetic considerations being largely irrelevant. But the onset of WWII, when all resources became focused on the war effort, brought a change of attitude. Rogerson, inspired by Pick, was already on his mission within ICI:

> '*…a good firm will risk damaging its public relations if its
> advertisements, the design of its buildings, the packeting
> of its goods are cheap, tawdry, or ugly… we persevered
> to persuade others that every ICI advertisement even
> in the least important trade journal must be as good
> as the best artist or photographer could make it.*'

And with war looming, Rogerson saw the use of good publicity for propaganda. In 1938 he brought out his manifesto, 'Propaganda in the Next War', an alert to the government of the need to rapidly establish a central body to meet, head on, the propaganda flooding in from Germany. Possibly as a result of his efforts he was appointed Advisor to the Army Council of the War Office, nominated to the position by Winston Churchill. That ICI was to continue to pay his salary, and that he was to combine his advisory work with his work in ICI, raised questions in the House as to conflict of interest, Hansard reporting that the issue was one of principle and not of person, as 'Mr. Rogerson's qualifications stand second to none'.

At ICI, Rogerson was not so much using 'unashamed' artists as making artists of repute feel 'unashamed' at lending their talents to publicising his company, which he described as 'morally fit and technically efficient'. And by contributing to the public image of ICI they also could be seen to be raising the reputation of the British chemical industry, overshadowed by that of Germany in the inter-war years. As some of these artists had rarely, if ever, previously done commercial work, Rogerson took it upon himself to give clear briefs, sometimes down to details, that he would not have needed to supply to full-blooded commercial artists. He described his relationship with his artists as 'a gay spirit of co-operation'.

The publicity outpourings from ICI took a variety of forms – improved exhibition stands, calendars illustrating ICI factories and laboratories [particularly for overseas customers], specifically focused advertising announcing a new product coming on to the market, and, from 1941, a number of 'series' for press advertisements. The first of these, 'Aspects of Industry', set out to show how other industries were dependent on the chemist.

There followed other series, for example 'Services of an Industry', demonstrating how the work of an industrial chemist affected everyday life – from the production of refrigerators to nylon stockings. The Rogerson series with perhaps the greatest impact was his 'Portraits of an Industry', for which artists such as the Zinkeisen sisters produced portraits of ICI employees, from those working on the shop floor to those in the boardroom, explaining the contribution of each to the war effort. With Kenneth Clark's encouragement, an exhibition of the portraits was mounted, first in London and then touring municipal galleries, later to be reproduced in a book.

There are few accounts of Rogerson's relationships with specific artists, the fullest being that given by Edward Wadsworth's daughter Barbara in her biography of her father. She describes the interest Rogerson took in her father, of Rogerson's visits to the family home to persuade Wadsworth to provide work for ICI. This turned out to be a 'godsend' because Wadsworth, at the time, was depressed and in poor health, and was grateful to have some 'real' work to do. He took commissions from Rogerson throughout the war, particularly for publicising new man-made dyes and processes, such as nylon and Perspex. Barbara recorded:

'The very fact that he had a deadline and a purpose sharpened his senses and helped him to do better things.'

Although Rogerson's publicity was primarily for selling, or rather announcing, new products, he saw much of it as 'giving expression to the personality of the company':

'I may say in perfect truth that if I did not honestly believe that ICI was a worthwhile show, a concern which was a national asset, I could not and indeed would not put my energies into trying to show people in Great Britain and the larger world overseas how good and efficient it is.'

That riding into battle, banners held high, Rogerson drew into his cohort a large number of artists is to his credit. The list includes not only the Zinkeisens and Wadsworth but Felix Kelly, Tom Purvis, John Tunnard, Frank Dobson, John Armstrong, and Charles F. Tunnicliffe. Henry Rushbury the architectural artist, also used by Rogerson, wrote in admiration:

'…the new patronage [industrial] supports with encouragement and sympathy and is repaid with gratitude. This achievement, in my view, must go to the credit of Sidney Rogerson…all ICI commissions with the art world bear the stamp of his personality.'

Rogerson retired to pursue his rural interests, but what followed can be attributed to his earlier enthusiasm and pioneering for improved industrial patronage of artists and designers. After Rogerson, ICI went on to impress even further with its publicity and advertising, as with Hans Schleger's dramatic images for Terylene, but that is another story.

EPILOGUE

orld War II was a watershed between the early generation of graphic designers and the generation to follow. The maestro, McKnight Kauffer, had returned to the United States in 1940. Several of the 'old school' were still active, Bateman, Newbould, Taylor, Fitton, Gentleman and Fougasse – making their particular contribution to the war effort by urging the population to save money, eat more healthily, dig their own vegetables and avoid careless talk. At the same time the war provided opportunities for the next generation to flower – George Him, Hans Schleger, Abram Games, Pat Keely, F.H.K. Henrion all provided posters advising people how to avoid the hazards of the blackout, asking them to be more economical in the use of the telephone, or encouraging women to 'join up'. Abram Games's ATS recruitment posters were some of the most iconic of the war period, and that Frank Newbould was reporting to him symbolised the changeover. This was to be further exemplified in the graphics for the Festival of Britain, with Games's Festival symbol to be seen just about everywhere, on everything, whilst Eric Fraser was commissioned to do colourful borders and black-and-white vignettes for the programme posters! By the late 1960s Taylor, Gentleman, Newbould, Purvis and Cooper were all dead, and the Zinkeisens had returned to portraiture and Fitton to his painting.

As McKnight Kauffer dominated the British graphic design scene in the inter-war years, so Games was to tower over poster design in the post-war years. But it was Schleger and Henrion who were to change the focus of commercial art; not content with the odd poster or press advertisement or packaging, they turned their talents to corporate identity design – co-ordinating, as far as practical, every visual aspect of an organisation from stationery to transport. Of course there had been earlier examples of 'corporate identity', notably for some of the London department stores, but Schleger's and Henrion's work was 'grown-up' stuff – negotiations at board level rather than with the publicity manager, involvement in organisational politics and with design management. Henrion, working with the Post Office, was to redesign some four hundred and fifty items; Schleger provided some seven hundred different designs in his seven years' work for MacFisheries.

Within forty years, the scene of academic artists providing grandiose pictures to which words were attached, and 'commercial' being considered a vulgar epithet when added to 'art', had given way to one where graphic designers could be given overall responsibility for how organisations presented themselves visually, and commercial art had achieved a professional status. 'Unashamed' artists had come of age.

REFERENCES

The bulk of the text and images have been drawn from
*Commercial Art/Art & Industry, The Penrose Annual, Modern
Publicity* and the supplement to the *Advertisers' Weekly.*

GENERAL TEXTS

1924 Walter Shaw Sparrow *Advertising in British Art* John Lane

c1925 Percy V. Bradshaw *Art in Advertising* The Press Art School

1927 R.P. Gossop *Advertising Design* Chapman & Hall Ltd.

2010 Paul Rennie *Modern British Posters* Black Dog Publishing

TEXTS ON SPECIFIC ASPECTS OF COMMERCIAL ART

1930 H. Stuart Menzies *Let's Forget Business* A & C Black Ltd.

1948 The United Steel Companies Ltd. *Trade Winds*

1954 G.H. Saxon Mills *There is a Tide: The Life and Work
of Sir William Crawford* William Heinemann

1955 Sir Stephen Tallents *The Projection of England* The Olen Press

1982 Donald R. Knight & Alan D. Sabey *The Lion Roars at Wembley:
The British Empire Exhibition* Barnard & Westwood

1983 *That's Shell that is!* catalogue Barbican Gallery

1990 Berry Ritchie *'A Touch of Class': The Story
of Austin Reed* James & James

1993 Lynda Morris & Robert Radford *The Story of AIA* MOMA, Oxford

1996 David Wainwright *The British Tradition:
Simpson – a World of Style* Quiller Press

2006 Ruth Artmosnky *Jack Beddington, the footnote man* Artmonsky Arts

2008 Alan Powers *Art & Print: The Curwen Story* Tate Publishing

2010 Ruth Artmonsky *Shipboard Style: Colin Anderson
of the Orient Line* Artmonsky Arts

2012 Ruth Artmonsky *The Pleasures of Printing* Artmonsky Arts

TEXTS ON, OR BY, SPECIFIC ARTISTS

1922 A.A. Milne [introduction] *Drawn at a Venture: A collection
of drawings by Fougasse* Methuen & Co. Ltd.

1924 E. McKnight Kauffer *The Art of the Poster* Cecil Palmer

1937 Tom Purvis *Poster Progress* The Studio Ltd.

1938 Austin Cooper *Making a Poster* The Studio Ltd.

1942 Francis Marshall *Fashion Drawing* The Studio Publications

1956 Ashley [Havinden] *Advertising and the Artist* The Studio Ltd.

1959 Francis Marshall *Magazine Illustration* The Studio Ltd.

1974 Alec Davis *Eric Fraser* The Uffculme Press

1977 Bevis Hillier *Fougasse* Elm Tree Books

1979 Mark Haworth-Booth *E. McKnight Kauffer* Gordon Fraser

1986 Edward Booth-Clibborn *André François* Polygon Editions

1987 *James Fitton R.A.1899–1982* catalogue Dulwich Picture Gallery

1998 Sylvia Backemeyer *Eric Fraser* Lund Humphries

2001 Pat Schleger *Hans Schleger, a life* Lund Humphries

2007 Brian Webb & Peyton Skipwith *E. McKnight Kauffer* ACC

2008 Philip Kelleway *Highly Desirable: The Zinkeisen
Sisters and their Legacy* Leiston Press

2011 Ruth Artmonsky & Brian Webb *F.H.K. Henrion* ACC

2011 Brian Webb & Peyton Skipwith *Claud Lovat Fraser* ACC

2011 The Estorick Collection *E. McKnight Kauffer* catalogue

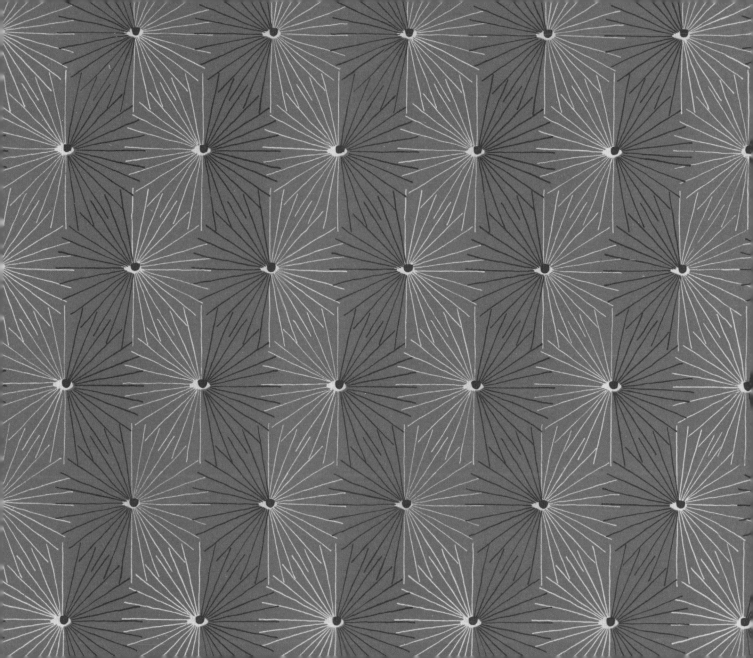